"*Called to Write* is a gift from Edna and Linda to every aspiring writer. Not many professionals are willing to share their trade secrets for success with others, especially those competing for the same market. Transparency to the extreme evidences their commitment to the ministry of writing.

"They teach that as a Christian writer you are not self-sufficient. Before you begin to write, know who God is and who you are. Then build your support team. At times, as you write, you will sense an unseen presence hovering over you. Relationships are essential if your words are going to change your readers. If you have a passion to write and the desire to become a published author, *Called to Write* is for you. Who you are in Christ will determine if you can write for Christ.

"Since most writers are not in a personal relationship with published authors, here is a great resource: In *Called to Write* you have more than a "how-to" or a "self-help" resource, you have the encouragement and inspiration of Edna and Linda with you as you write. With their help you can determine that you will write with excellence. That is what your readers will expect. As you write, anticipate by faith the blessing of your inspiration to write on your readers. If you have a story, use this book to share it as a published author."

—JACK SHAW, author of two books, member of the Central Committee
   of the Southern Baptist Convention and the Baptist Foundation, SBC

Other New Hope books by these authors

Love Notes in Lunch Boxes: And Other Ideas to Color Your Child's Day
by Linda Gilden

Deeper Still: A Woman's Study to a Closer Walk with God by Edna Ellison

Stronger Still: A Woman's Guide to Turning Your Hurt into Healing for Others
by Edna Ellison

Friend to Friend: Enriching Friendships Through a Shared Study of Philippians
by Edna Ellison

Friendships of Faith: A Shared Study of Hebrews by Edna Ellison

Friendships of Purpose: A Shared Study of Ephesians by Edna Ellison

Major Truths from Minor Prophets: Power, Freedom, and Hope for Women
by Edna Ellison, Tricia Scribner, and Kimberly Sowell

A Month of Miracles: 30 Stories of the Unmistakable Presence of God
by Edna Ellison, Kimberly Sowell, Joy Brown, Tricia Scribner,
Marie Alston, and Cherie Nettles

A Passion for Purpose: 365 Daily Devotions for Missional Living
by Edna Ellison, Kimberly Sowell, Joy Brown,
Tricia Scribner, and Marie Alston

Woman to Woman: Preparing Yourself to Mentor
by Edna Ellison and Tricia Scribner

Chosen and Cherished: Becoming the Bride of Christ
by Edna Ellison, Joy Brown, and Kimberly Sowell

Women of the Covenant: Spiritual Wisdom from Women of the Bible
by Edna Ellison and Kimberly Sowell

Called to
WRITE

SEVEN PRINCIPLES TO BECOME
A WRITER ON MISSION

Edna *Linda*
ellison & gilden

Called to
WRITE

SEVEN PRINCIPLES TO BECOME
A WRITER ON MISSION

NEW HOPE
P U B L I S H E R S
Gospel-Centered. Missions-Driven.

BIRMINGHAM, ALABAMA

New Hope® Publishers
P. O. Box 12065
Birmingham, AL 35202-2065
NewHopeDigital.com
New Hope Publishers is a division of WMU®.

Library of Congress Cataloging-in-Publication Data
Ellison, Edna.
  Called to write : 7 principles to become a writer on mission / Edna Ellison, Linda
Gilden.
    pages cm
  ISBN 978-1-59669-398-2 (sc)
  1. Authors--Prayers and devotions. 2. Authors--Religious life. 3. Authorship--
Religious aspects--Christianity. I. Title.
  BV4596.A85E45 2013
  248.8'8--dc23

                    2013037395

All Scripture quotations, unless otherwise indicated, are from the HOLY BIBLE:
NEW INTERNATIONAL VERSION®. NIV®. Copyright © 1973, 1978, 1984 by
Biblica. Used by permission. All rights reserved worldwide.

Scripture quotations marked KJV are taken from The Holy Bible, King James
Version.

Scripture quotations marked NLT are taken from the Holy Bible, New Living
Translation, copyright © 1996. Used by permission of Tyndale House Publishers,
Inc., Wheaton, Illinois. All rights reserved.

Cover and interior design by Glynese Northam

ISBN -10: 1-59669-398-3
ISBN-13: 978-1-59669-398-2
N144107 · 0314 · 2.5MI

Dedication

To think that a book would be written and produced by one single person is not an accurate thought. Anytime I write a book, I have a whole team of people who are right with me all the way.

Of course, my family. They support, encourage, cheer, and even do a little research when necessary. They endure Sunday lunches that are picked up rather than home cooked. They understand when I arrive to babysit with computer in hand. They don't give me any dirty looks when my bed is unmade or the laundry is piled up. They know the life of a writer and have been my head cheering squad all the way.

Thank you to each one of my precious family. John, you and the children and grandchildren join me in the ministry and blessing of this book. Every life that it touches will be a touch from you as well.

I have wanted to write this book for years. May God take it and use it according to His plan for many to become writers on mission.

Linda

Like Linda, I want to thank my family who are the joy of my life. To Jack, the best son anyone could have, and Patsy, the best daughter anyone could have, to my two in-laws, Tim and Wendy, the best spouses anyone could ask for her adult children, with patience to love their *ogre mother-in-law.* They always welcome me as Mimi in their lives. I appreciate their long-suffering and support as I write for extended periods of time.

Blakely, my intelligent, one-and-only granddaughter, is wonderful and greatly loved. She is my inspiration and a good writer herself already! My two granddogs, Willie and Frankie, have given me good breaks from the nose-to-the-grindstone writing sessions. I'm grateful for them as comic relief!

This book has been a joy to write. God absolutely gave us daily manna of inspiration and nudged us along when we ran out of ideas or lived in a time crunch from day to day. His Spirit refreshed us, and we are eternally grateful for His presence in our lives.

Table of Contents

Foreword

I really like this book. The basic thesis is simple but profound — "You can change the world through your words." When I first read the title, I assumed this book would be a great resource for aspiring or experienced writers. What I soon came to see is that this book is for every follower of Christ who wants to be a missional writer. The point is simple but profound. Followers of Christ have a story to tell and we must tell it well. Whether your goal is to publish or simply communicate your story more effectively, you need to read this book.

The early chapters will challenge you to look at your spiritual walk and write from the overflow of your own personal relationship with Christ. Edna Ellison and Linda Gilden provide numerous suggestions to improve your personal Bible study and quiet time with the aim of becoming a more effective missional communicator. The opening chapters are worth the price of the book as they challenge us to go deeper and give us practical suggestions for doing so.

Our authors indicate that the only valid reason to write is to glorify the King and thus advance His kingdom. Since I have been privileged to write several books, I am frequently asked about writing and publishing. I am quick to warn aspiring writers that it is hard work, but that it is worth the effort if you are compelled by the Spirit to write. Our authors would agree, but they do more than give encouragement; they provide practical tips about writing and publishing. The instructions on the craft of writing and editing are as helpful as you will find in any book in the field. I am delighted to have a resource to put in the hands of those who ask me how to get started or how to get better when it comes to a writing ministry.

This book will provide you with more than you expect. Just scan the table of contents and you will see that it goes beyond the typical book on writing and being published. Here are a few of my favorites: "How to Write with Christ Perspective," "The Influential Stage of Writing for Christ," "How to Write Through Personal Relationships," "How to Know and Reach Your Audience," and "How to Write Under Christ's Leadership."

This is one book you must read to the very last page. The concluding section, which offers an interview with our authors, is invaluable. Not only do they share themselves with us, but they provide a unique summary that will help us practice the principles found in the book. They bring everything down to seven simple keys—spirituality, Scripture study, worldview, relationships, communication, ministry, and leadership.

If you are reading this brief foreword because you have just purchased this volume, enjoy. If you are still trying to decide whether you need another book or your first book on writing, buy it, read it, and practice it. You will learn how to live and write missionally.

Ken Hemphill

AUTHOR OF MORE THAN 35 BOOKS, DIRECTOR OF THE CENTER FOR CHURCH PLANTING AND REVITALIZATION AT NORTH GREENVILLE UNIVERSITY

Preface

Many years ago, God called us to be writers. Our experiences were different but our calling was the same—"Write for Me (God)."

One of us was called at a conference through a series of unusual circumstances and went kicking and screaming into the writing world. The other had wanted to be a writer all her life but stepped away from the dream because of the discouragement of a college professor and took years to resume her writing journey. Despite the differences in the way we were called, we find great similarities in the way we have lived out our calling as Christian writers. If you asked us to describe what it is like to be a Christian writer, we would probably respond in unison, "Wonderful!" We love what we do and feel blessed beyond measure to spend our days writing the messages God has given us.

Because we feel secure in what we do and are excited to be used of God in this way, we want to encourage other Christian writers. Writing is a very lonely vocation. You sit for hours at a computer in a room all by yourself and don't talk to anyone. Your inspiration comes from God as you write. There are times you feel isolated and alone. But the things we learn as we sit and listen for God's direction are beyond measure. God loves for writers to surrender their careers to Him and let Him direct. Relinquishing control is not always an easy thing to do. We struggle with that just like every other Christian writer.

This book is not about the struggle of being a Christian writer. It is more about the blessing of following God's call to be a writer on His team. Nothing is more fun and exciting than knowing what God's plan is for your life and following His plan.

As you read this book, we hope you will be affirmed if you are seeking God's plan for your life, encouraged if you have discovered He has called you to be a writer, blessed if you are already on a long writing journey and can say a hearty "Amen!" to everything in the book. Thank you for allowing us to be part of this journey with you. We have already prayed for you and will continue to do so. We hope you will do the same for us.

May every word you write make a difference for His kingdom!

Edna and Linda

Acknowledgments

Most books have an acknowledgement section at the beginning. And they all sound very similar. That's because all writers know that the production of a book takes more than just their efforts. This book is no different.

Thanks to New Hope Publishers, who believed in us and in the message of this book. We appreciate so much publisher Andrea Mullins and Joyce Dinkins and her team of editors and designers. Thank you, our publishers on mission, for your strong guidance and support. You are the best!

Thanks to our families. We know how hard it is to have a writer in the family. It requires sacrifice on your parts that doesn't go unnoticed. We love you and thank you for your prayers, cheers, and unwavering love.

Introduction

What does it mean to be "on mission"? Some use the word *missional.*

The dictionary lists multiple meanings for the word *mission.* The one most applicable to this book is "a strongly felt aim, ambition, or calling." The origin of the word in the middle of the sixteenth century comes from the Latin meaning "to send," specifically denoting the sending of the Holy Spirit.

So how do you know if you are called to be a writer? Does God whisper it in your ear or speak it through a friend? Did He give you a story that begs to be shared? Did He give you a story He's nudging you to write? Some writers have known for a long time that writing was their passion and they have second-grade essays to prove it. Others dabbled along in other activities collecting great material before discovering the pure joy in knowing God's direction for their lives.

Answering the question of How do you really know? is a personal matter. The answer can come only from God. Seeking that answer can take hours of prayer, soul-searching, and counsel. Look deeply in your heart and find your true desires. Yield your life to God and watch how He leads you. Are doors opening that could be only His doing? Are there opportunities presented to you that could be only divine intervention?

Once you have established your calling and feel God's direction to write, you know what your goal is: to be the best writer you can be and to write for Him with excellence. You may not write full-time, especially in the beginning, but whatever opportunity you have to write, you must approach it with the same dedication and commitment.

Being on mission or missional is to be focused. To have your sights set on a goal and work unwaveringly to reach that goal. To feel so passionate about your calling you work tirelessly to communicate your message to others.

As writers who are believers, our message is clear. We write to bring honor to our Lord and Savior Jesus Christ. That doesn't mean that every word, article, or book we write must be a sermon. That doesn't mean that everything we write must be evangelistic. However, it does mean that everything we write, no matter what the subject, should be written with excellence and in a way that honors our Lord.

Christian writers need to write about every subject, even those that seem to be "secular." The world needs writers who are on mission to bring hope to those who feel none. Missional writers need to be the bright spot in a reader's otherwise dreary day.

So let's move forward in our calling to be the very best writers we can be. After all, we have the very best message—a message of hope for a hurting world.

"If you want to change the world, pick up a pen."
—MARTIN LUTHER

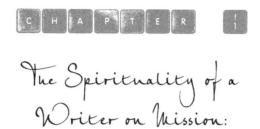

The Spirituality of a Writer on Mission:

WRITING FROM THE OVERFLOW—THE FIRST STAGE OF WRITING FOR CHRIST

This is what we speak not in words taught us by human wisdom but in words taught by the Spirit, expressing spiritual truths in spiritual words.

1 CORINTHIANS 2:13

I'm sure you have heard the cliché "Is the glass half empty or half full?" But what about the glass that is full, even to the point of overflowing? Luke 6:45 says, "Out of the overflow of the heart the mouth speaks." Can't we paraphrase that verse to read, "Out of the overflow of the heart the pen writes?"

Unless we write from an overflow of our relationship with Jesus Christ, our words are empty and have little eternal value. To write meaningful books, articles, poems, and other manuscripts, we must have something of value to share.

One morning Karyn sat on the porch as the sun was coming up. She was alone, enjoying watching the day put on its brilliant colors. Karyn looked at the swimming pool in the backyard, so still, looking as if the surface was highly polished glass.

As the sun made its way over the hill, the light caused a crystal-clear reflection of the trees lined up around the perimeter of the property. In the pool was a perfect mirror image of what was around it.

Sitting there Karyn realized there was a reason the pool could reflect like that. *That pool has a clear image of the things around it because of what is in it,* she thought. The pool is full to the top with water and the water is reflecting the beauty around it.

Isn't that the way it is with your relationship with God? If you are full of Him, not half full but totally filled up, you will reflect His love and light to the world. Those around you will see His beauty reflected from the Living Water that fills you. Whether you are writing, speaking, or chatting with someone in the grocery store, His love and light will be reflected.

Each of us must pay attention and nurture our relationship with God. To become a writer on mission we must work hard to fill ourselves with His love that can overflow to those around us and reflect the kingdom in everything we write, say, or do!

How does a writer build a relationship with God that allows him or her to be filled to overflowing?

THE SPIRITUALITY OF A WRITER ON MISSION

Spirituality is a pretty heavy word. But pure and simple, the spirituality of a writer refers to his or her relationship with God. That in itself is not pure and simple. But it is the one thing that will determine whether or not a writer is on mission or writes from some other motivation.

What is the basis or springboard for what you write? Where do you get your ideas, but more importantly, what motivates your ideas?

For the Christian writer, ideas should spring from his or her Christian worldview. How do you view the world in light of your faith? How do you look at others because you love Jesus? What is your response to tragedy and trauma? Do you want to run from suffering or do you immediately begin to pray for its alleviation?

Can the depth of concern for the hearts and salvation of your readers cause you to drop tears on your keyboard?

Where do you begin? Regardless of whether or not you are a writer, your relationship with God begins with birth. You don't actually have a relationship with Him when you are born. You are focused on you. But He has created you and His purpose in creating you is to have a relationship with Him. So He wants you to grow into that relationship and come to the point of asking Him to be Lord of your life.

As we grow as people and begin to take in our surroundings, we become aware of the beauty around us. We may not even know it but we become aware of a creation that could only be the work of the Master Creator. As we get older and our understanding increases, we become aware of the sin not only in the world but in our own lives. At some point we must come face-to-face with the fact that we are sinners. Perhaps your parents were the first to tell you that you were not perfect. Or maybe your Sunday School teacher took the time to explain in depth what it means to be a sinner and how Jesus died on the Cross for you.

In whatever way you came to know the Lord, He has now called you to be a writer to point others to Him. Once you have experienced and accepted His salvation, you are His messenger to the world. From the point of salvation on, you are preparing to be the best messenger you can be.

First Peter 3:15 says, "Always be prepared to give an answer to everyone who asks you to give the reason for the hope that you have. But do this with gentleness and respect." *Always* is pretty clear, isn't it? Whether we are in the grocery store line or at our computers, we should be spreading His message.

Many think they can write inspirational pieces as long as they mention some sort of faith. But the faith that is going to change lives is that which springs from the writer's relationship with God.

Second Timothy 2:15 says, "Do your best to present yourself to God as one approved, a workman who does not need to be ashamed and who correctly handles the word of truth." When I was a child, I learned that verse in another translation and it reads, "Study to show thyself approved" (KJV).

Once we accept Jesus Christ into our lives, we embark on a lifelong journey of learning, learning that affects every area of our lives. We read the Bible, listen to sermons, pray, and spend time listening to God so we can get to know Him better. In the beginning we don't even know the magnitude of our study and how it will affect our lives. But as we begin to develop our relationships with God and get to know Him and experience His amazing love, we realize our faith in God is going to influence every aspect of our lives.

Of all the many facets to growing a relationship with God, one is not more important than the other. They could happen in any order. Let's look at a few of the most important things to engage in and grow as Christian writers on mission.

STUDY

As Timothy mentioned above, we must study. In this case and in our positions as writers, that study must first and foremost be studying the Word of God.

Do you have a quiet time every day? Do you designate a time to read your Bible and search for the message God has just for you? Or is the only time you really get into the Word when your pastor says, "Please turn in your Bibles to . . . Daily Bible study is vital for every Christian. We have a responsibility to dig deeply and understand the message God has for us. But as writers, our responsibility goes a little further. We need to study, understand, and internalize the Word of God in a way that we can let it overflow into the lives of others through our writing.

What is the best method of studying the Bible? That is somewhat personal. You need to find the method of Bible study that works best for you.

Hannah tends to remember things much better when she writes them down. So for her, a system where she reads a passage, asks God to show her His wisdom in the passage, then writes it in a journal, notebook, or the computer works best. Sometimes she just writes freely, not really connecting the dots until later but knowing there is purpose in the time she is spending in study.

So "study to show yourself approved" as Timothy says in 2 Timothy 2:15. Why do Christian writers need to study? After all, they are the ones writing all the materials for others to read, aren't they? Yes, but unless the writer has studied and filled himself or herself up with God's Word, nothing of eternal value will overflow on the pages.

> *"The battle is lost or won in the secret places of the will before God, never first in the external world."*
> —OSWALD CHAMBERS

 PRAYER

Prayer is all important in our relationships with God. Sometimes our conversations with God need to be long and deep. At other times, we have time to breathe only a quick prayer of acknowledgment of His presence.

When Toni has a new neighbor move into her neighborhood, she quickly plans a time she can go over to visit and get to know him or her. If Toni remains in her comfortable home and never makes the effort to learn all she can about her new neighbor, Toni will never know what the neighbor is like. Toni won't know about her family, the things that are important to her, what makes her the way she is, and on and on.

As they get to know each other better, Toni and her neighbor develop a relationship, a friendship that will serve them well during good times and bad. When her neighbor has a joy, Toni wants to rush next door and tell her. When something is troubling Toni, her neighbor is the first one she asks to pray for her. That close relationship is possible because they have gotten to know each other through conversations.

God conversations are important. He wants to hear what we have to say. He wants to know what we think are our most critical needs (even though He knows before we ask) and how we think they should be met. He wants us to pour out the desires of our hearts to Him. Our constant conversation with God will increase awareness of His presence and reliance on Him in every situation.

Another important aspect of our prayer is listening. Often we forget that listening is part of the prayer experience; we run to God with our lists of needs but then say, "Amen!" and resume life without ever listening for His answers. You are probably thinking that God doesn't answer our prayers the minute we pray them. Maybe not always. But often we end our prayer sessions when we finish our prayers without even giving God a chance to respond. Then we cry that He never answers us or takes too long to do so.

Listening prayer needs to be part of our everyday prayers. Once we finish our petitions and have emptied our hearts of our concerns, then we are ready to listen to what God has in store for us.

Does He speak audibly during these listening sessions? He can. But more often than not He speaks in that still small voice that whispers deep within our hearts. It is the sudden assurance of knowing exactly what to do in a situation, what to say to a friend, or whether or not a decision should be yes or no.

As Christian writers we not only need to pray, we need to be prayed for. One of the best things Liz ever did for herself and her writing career was to develop a prayer team. Liz felt the need for others to be able to pray specifically regarding her speaking and writing needs. About once a month or every six weeks, Liz creates a calendar for the prayer team and sends it out with specific needs. She includes speaking engagements, writing deadlines, and personal requests. She feels so much more confident when she knows God is hearing not only from her but also from those who love and support her ministry. Often when Liz is on the road she will receive a call or text delivering a prayer from one of her prayer team. If you have someone who keeps your calendar for you or an assistant who helps with your ministry, the prayer calendar could be one of his or her responsibilities.

"Pray without ceasing" (1 Thessalonians 5:17). What does this mean to a writer? It means stay in constant contact with the One who cares the most about your writing. Talk to Him when you get an idea for a project. Let Him guide you as you do your research. Trust Him to lead you to the right publisher and agent for your work. Relinquish your work to Him and see what He will do with it! After all, you are writing it for Him. He wants people to read it as much as you do!

> *"The truth is, we can do great things after we pray, but we cannot do great things until we pray."*
> (THE DAILY ENCOURAGING WORD, FEBRUARY 25, 2013).

RELATIONSHIPS

Later on in the book we will discuss relationships. But we must mention relationships as we talk about the spirituality of the writer. Relationships are important as our faith spills over into everything we do.

We have been zeroing in on the primary relationship of every Christian, the relationship with our heavenly Father. That should be our primary focus. But the relationships around us are also important. Whom do we hang out with? When we need a friend, do we turn to a Christian brother or will anyone with a listening ear do?

The Bible tells us to go out into the world. That is important. But when we seek relationships that can point us to the Father and draw us closer to Him, we need to find a Christian brother or sister who can hold us accountable and help us learn more about the God we serve.

So seek out good relationships. Find one special person who can hold you accountable. Perhaps you can find a writer friend and you can hold yourselves mutually accountable not only for your spiritual focus but also for your writing deadlines. This is a tremendous help when deadlines loom and time seems to get away from you. Just having someone who really knows how you feel and can truly empathize makes your burden lighter.

God can speak to us through our relationships. We may think the message comes from the wisdom of a friend, but that is not the case. It is God's wisdom spoken through a friend. God uses us to be His messengers in many ways—to speak wisdom to a friend, to counsel those around us, or to write His message so that many others can know His truth.

WORSHIP

"Therefore, I urge you brothers, in view of God's mercy, to offer your bodies as living sacrifices, holy and pleasing to God—this is your spiritual act of worship" (ROMANS 12:1).

What do you think of when you hear the word *worship*? Sacrifice is probably not the first thing that comes to mind, but that is what Paul tells us is our spiritual act of worship—sacrifice of our bodies and everything we do. Although *sacrifice* is not a word we hear often in our world today, we can provide a definition that will cover all our bases. Sacrifice as a spiritual act of worship is submitting everything—all of your wishes, needs, desires, hopes, and dreams— to come under the blood of Jesus. As you filter the things of the world into your life, it becomes an act of worship before God as you follow His guidance to respond to the world.

Growing up, *worship* was heard more as a noun than as a verb. "Are you going to worship today?" "What are we going to do after worship is over?" And, of course, going to worship and attending church services is very important.

But as you get older and deepen your relationship with God, you realize that Paul was exactly right. You can attend worship weekly at your churches and enjoy corporately praising the Father and studying His Word together, but the kind of worship that has the deepest significance in our lives is the worship where we are oblivious to the world and lift our spirits to God, seeking oneness with Him.

Personally, writing can be one of the primary acts of worship in the day. You can be constantly aware of God's presence in your writing day. Selma often has praise music going in the background and pauses often just to give Him her undivided attention. She is deeply aware of His love and provision and guidance as she writes. Definitely, writing for Him is worship.

> *"Writing can be one of the primary acts of worship in the day."*

WORLDVIEW

Think back to before you knew Christ. What were your deepest thoughts about the world? How did you respond to tragedy, delight, new experiences? Did you ever consider there was Someone watching over you? When you needed a friend, whom did you turn to? Who did you think created this amazing world?

Before we meet Jesus, we have no basis for connecting the dots in the world. In fact, we have no basis for anything. Everything just exists and we have no idea where it came from. Once we realize God created the world and everything in it has a purpose, we look at the whole world through different eyes. We have God inside us and we view everything through His eyes.

Colors are brighter, flowers are more beautiful, children are more precious, friends are closer, and our attitudes are more loving. We begin to view the world as God views it, something precious to be treasured and sought after. He created the world and each of us to have fellowship with Him. Even after sin came into the world, He didn't give up on His purpose for us. He sent His only Son to die for us. What love! What love!

That love becomes a part of us when we accept Jesus' forgiveness through His blood and ask Him to come into our hearts and lives. After that point, everything will be filtered through God's love. As we regard the world through the eyes of God, so should everything we write have the same filter and reflect the love of God. Surely every word does not have to be about God, but everything should be backed up with a view that reflects and honors Him.

When a writer who is a Christian writes, he or she writes with an awareness that God is at work all around. He or she acknowledges what an incredible blessing it is to be a kingdom writer, someone who can point others to Christ with the words on paper.

God may not call you to write a best seller if He has even called you to be successful in the eyes of other people. But God is pleased when you share His message in print and help others learn to do the same.

In the movie *Chariots of Fire*, Eric Liddell addressed his sister's concerns about the Olympics interfering with his missionary career in China with this statement: "When I run, I feel God's pleasure." He understood the importance of fulfilling the purpose God had planned for him rather than being successful in the eyes of others.

You may remember times when you understood the extreme power of words. Whether writing or teaching, you want your words to point others to the purpose God intends for them.

You may not be a runner, but when you write and invest in the lives of other writers, do you feel God's pleasure?

THE MISSIONARY IN YOU

1 Do you have balance in your spiritual life?
2 Every morning, do you ask God to show you someone with whom you can share the gospel either by word of mouth or word of pen?
3 Isaiah 61:3 says, "You are a planting of the Lord for the display of His splendor." Could you display His splendor with your words in print?
4. Could your message impact lives for the kingdom?

THE WRITER IN YOU

1. What is it that you do that makes you feel God's pleasure?
2. Do you love being a writer? What do you like most about answering God's call on your life?
3. Are you filling your "cup" daily from the Word of God and spending time with Him so that you can overflow onto the pages of your work and into the world?
4. Do you feel personally rejected when a manuscript is turned down? Or can you receive it as another open door for ministry in a different area?

A WRITER'S PRAYER

Dear God, You are the author of my faith. I want to read well the plan You have for me and absorb it into my heart and life in a way that others want what I have. Make me faithful to the calling You have given me and give me peace and determination along the way. I know writing is a lot of sometimes unrewarded work. The only reward I need is to know You are pleased with what I write. I want You to receive honor for everything I write. Amen.

CHAPTER 2

The Basics of Writing from Spiritual Growth

DIGGING DEEPLY—HOW TO GROW IN CHRIST

For this reason, since the day we heard about you, we have not stopped praying for you. We continually ask God to fill you with the knowledge of his will through all the wisdom and understanding that the Spirit gives, so that you may live a life worthy of the Lord and please him in every way: bearing fruit in every good work, growing in the knowledge of God.

COLOSSIANS 1:9–10

Developing a relationship with God is important no matter what your profession and even if you have no profession. God created you for a relationship with Him and that should come before any career aspiration or choice.

As Christian writers, spiritual growth needs to take priority. Writers are responsible to their readers. Our loyal following of readers depend on us. As leaders in Christian ministry, we need to assume that responsibility, prepare for it, and take it seriously.

Most children can't wait to grow up. They beg their parents for privileges long before they are ready for them.

"I can't wait until I am 16 and can drive a car."

"Why can't I wear makeup *now*?"

"I want a sharp knife just like my daddy!"

Physical and emotional growth is a normal pattern of life. It happens whether we are ready or prepared for it or not.

HOW TO GROW IN CHRIST

Some people think spiritual growth happens naturally, especially if they are regular church attenders. But just showing up at church once a week doesn't necessarily promote solid, lasting spiritual growth. Growing spiritually, deepening your relationship with our heavenly Father, must be intentional. You have to work to make it happen.

 FOCUS

Unlike physical growth, it is difficult to measure spiritual growth. Many of the markers are internal and between you and God. Certainly you can see from people's actions whether or not they love God. But spiritual growth is determined in the heart.

One way to focus is to choose a theme verse each year. Ask God to show you what He wants you to focus on from His Word and start with one verse. Write the verse on index cards and keep them in your purse and car. When you have 30 seconds in a checkout line, read your verse. When the traffic light turns red, read your verse. Use that verse as wallpaper on your phone or computer where you will see it daily. Put it by the sink so you can read it a few times while you are washing dishes or in the bathroom while you are brushing your teeth. Enclose it in a plastic bag and hang in the shower. Repeating your verse over and over will help you memorize it in a very short time. If you find memorization difficult, try putting your verse to music and singing it repeatedly.

A few suggestions for theme verses are Isaiah 26:3, Philippians 4:13, Psalm 119:32, Galatians 5:16, Jeremiah 29:11, or Joshua 1:9. Find a verse that speaks specifically to what you would like to accomplish for God in the current year. Your theme verse will change every year and before long you will have committed many verses to memory.

Develop a mission statement for your ministry. You may say, "This doesn't apply to me because I don't have an official ministry." Has God called you to be a writer? Do you have a message you feel compelled to communicate to the world? Do you have a hard time passing by the computer without working on a book, article, or blog?

If you have felt the call of God on your life, you have a ministry and you need to focus on just what your mission is. A mission statement should be short enough to remember and long enough to say exactly what you feel called to do. Be sure to make it specific because your mission statement will be a measuring rod for everything you do in ministry. There is so much good to be done and so many people to reach for Christ. But one person cannot do it all. Focus on what God has called you to do and pray for those who have been called to do other things.

If God has called you to be a writer, your mission statement might read something like this: "My mission is to reach as many as I can for Christ through the print media, especially articles and nonfiction books, striving to make a difference in the life of every reader."

Or it may read something like this: "God has called me to craft stories that contain truth in everyday life that will entertain and delight fiction readers and point them to Jesus."

Whatever you choose, realize you can use that statement to decide whether or not to write something someone has asked you to do. For instance, if your church comes to you and says, "We need our church history book updated. We think you should do it because you are such a great and talented writer." Does that fit either of the mission statements above? It may work with the first, but it definitely will not work with statement number two.

Does that mean you should not write a book for your church? No, it doesn't mean that at all. We should tithe our talent as well as our financial means. But unless you are the only writer in the church, there may be someone who is much better suited to that job than you. If you have a particular interest in the church history and after praying feel that the job is something God wants you to do, by all means, put your heart into it and do the very best job you can. But if you are maxed out timewise and have many deadlines pending, you are justified in turning down that position. If God has given you a mission and you have a concise statement to help you stay focused, then you know what it is you need to do with your time each day.

Writing can be a solitary calling. An important part of spiritual growth is fellowship with others. For sure we could grow if we lived on a deserted island and spent every moment with God. But God tells us in Hebrews 10:25 not to give up meeting together. He created us for fellowship with Him, but that doesn't mean He intended us to be reclusive. He created us as social beings and we need each other. We can learn from each other and as we see Jesus in the lives of those around us, we are encouraged to be His hands and feet here on earth.

> *"If you have felt the call of God on your life, you have a ministry and you need to focus on just what your mission is."*

   READ

Of course, the obvious answer here is to read the Bible. We know God's Word is where we can find Him and get to know His heart. We can go to His book anytime and anywhere to find answers to life's deepest questions, fellowship with our loving heavenly Father, or rest in the peace it brings to our lives.

If you are industrious and like a strong regimen, try reading the entire Bible through in a year. There are many print and online resources that provide a plan for doing this. Your church may even have a plan for your church family to do this together. If you have already read the Bible through, choose a different translation and start all over. If you don't like to follow someone else's plan, create your own. Make a chart so you know you don't leave any part out. Any method that works for you is a good place to start.

Perhaps reading the entire Bible feels a little like eating a whole elephant. The saying goes that there is only one way to eat the elephant—one bite at a time. So perhaps you need to take just a "bite" of the Bible when you first begin to study.

Choose one book of the Bible to study. There are study guides available on every book in the Bible. Invest in one of them, get a fresh notebook, and dive in. Choose the time frame that works best for you—once a month, once a quarter, or even one book for the year.

Read good books by authors who will encourage you in your faith. Read both fiction and nonfiction. Explore different genres to learn from authors of all types of writing. Make note of spiritual truths that are in all types of writing. Observe how other people approach their faith and grow in response to life situations.

Pick a topic to read about. Study what God's Word says about it and read your Bible as well as solid books on the topic. Determine weak areas in your relationship with God and read books that will help you overcome them.

Writers tend to read a lot as well as write. So what's on your reading list for the coming year? Or do you even have a reading list? It helps to plan those things you read that are apart from your writing research. If you write nonfiction, yet love escaping into the take-me-away world of fiction, let reading time be your reward for a good, productive day of writing.

PRAY

There is no substitute for spending time in prayer. Just as conversations with an acquaintance brings him or her into a closer relationship with you, conversations with God will deepen your friendship with Him and help you get to know Him on a more personal basis. As a Christian writer, you write for God. So isn't it a good idea to talk to Him about your writing?

If you don't have a plan for regular "visits" with God, stop right now and develop one. Write it down. Take into consideration your daily schedule. We often hear that we should start the day with an hour or so of quiet time. That may work for someone who is a morning person and doesn't have children to get off to school or a job to get to. But for most of us, life begins very quickly once the sun comes up. So take a few minutes to assess if first thing in the morning is really the best time for you to have some time alone with God.

If you stay at home during the day, you may want to wait until the house has cleared out and everyone else has gone to jobs and school. If you have a full-time job, you may find you can spend your lunch break munching your sandwich in some quiet corner of a restaurant or the breakroom while you read your Bible and have a time of prayer. If you have a houseful of preschoolers or toddlers, you may want to wait until naptime or after the children are tucked in bed. There is no right or wrong time to spend time with God. Making sure it is a time you can focus on Him and give Him your full attention is the most important thing.

It is beneficial to pray with and for others. Find several other writers who would like to join you and set up a regular time to meet and pray and encourage each other. This does not have to be a long, drawn-out meeting. But knowing you have the prayer support of others who know what your life is like trying to meet deadlines and write books can be a tremendous boost to your confidence.

Prayer support for your ministry is a must. A prayer team is also an essential part of your ministry. Although it was mentioned earlier, it bears mentioning again. Gather together some friends who are willing to pray for you and then make sure they have the information they need to pray specifically for your ministry needs.

> "*Without exception the men and women I have known who made the most rapid, consistent, and evident growth in Christlikeness have been those who develop a daily time of being alone with God. This time of outward silence is the time of daily Bible intake and prayer. In this solitude is the occasion for private worship.*"
>
> —DONALD WHITNEY, *Spiritual Disciplines for the Christian Life*

 JOURNAL

These days journaling is a very popular form of worship. Worship? Yes, worship.

As you write your thoughts and prayers, you are creating yet another method to communicate with your heavenly Father.

Many of us had diaries when we were younger, places to write our deepest thoughts where they were safe from anyone else. We wrote in them every day and then locked them back and secured the key around our necks.

What is the difference in a journal and a diary? A journal is a place to record happenings. You might write in it every day or you might write once a week. You might use it to record your thoughts about a certain passage of Scripture. But isn't a diary the same thing? The journal and the diary are similar and come in all sizes and forms. The important thing is that either of them provides you with a place to record your life's experiences and gives you a way to look back on your life's journey and growth pattern. You can see what God has done in your life.

When you write in your journal, you will discover things about yourself. Your journal will help you generate ideas; it will become a good friend and confidant.

You can use your journal to:

1. Preserve memories. One year Sherri had a child from India to live in her home. The child was ten at the time and immediately fit into Sherri's family. The experience leading up to the child arriving was a pretty neat story. Sherri wrote it in her journal because the story showed what a God-journey it was. While her Indian daughter was in Sherri's home, all three of the girls (Sherri had two girls of her own that were joined by her Indian daughter) wanted Sherri to read that story for their bedtime story every night. It was important to her family to have a record of God's hand in that part of their lives.

2. Write down your innermost thoughts. Everyone needs someone to confide in. Someone they feel safe with. For many people that "someone" is their journal.

3. Encourage others. God will bring circumstances into the lives of others that are similar to things you have experienced. If you have written them down and recorded the answers God gave to get through the situation, you can refer to your journal to assist you in remembering and ministering to others.

4. Deepen your relationship with God. As God teaches you through Bible study, prayer, and experiencing Him through the lives of others, you will benefit from jotting down those lessons. You can also write prayers instead of speaking them aloud. Many beautiful prayers that have been published started out on the pages of a journal.

As a writer, can a journal really benefit you, or is it taking time away from your writing?

Keeping a journal can help you sort through your life's experiences. Many times we find ourselves in situations we don't understand. But when we get through them, we realize the things God was teaching us and can share the story with others to help them. Writing in a journal can help us sort through emotions and put aside things that are concerning us, thereby freeing us to write. Journaling can be therapeutic and healing. Getting our emotions and deepest feelings out helps us as we become the person God made us to be.

HOW CAN YOUR JOURNAL BENEFIT YOU AS A WRITER?

Personally, your journal can be a gold mine. You can discover what God is saying to you. Through your entries, you will see how He is working in your life and how He brought you from point A to point B. You will understand yourself better as you see your actions and reactions to difficult and trying events. You can sense your joy through uplifting times.

Professionally, a journal can be a treasure trove of information and rich stories to make your writing come alive. You can use the entries to spur ideas for articles. If you see one theme emerging in a number of entries, you may want to consider writing a book. You can write devotions and columns and submit to compilation books. You will have a wealth of material to share with others for their encouragement and spiritual growth.

Jennifer's family has an annual tradition of making jelly. One year they had so much fun Jennifer took time to write extensively about the experience in her journal. That entry became an article in a national magazine and an entry in about a half dozen books!

These days there are many options for journaling. In the past when you thought about journaling, a pen and notebook immediately came to mind. But now, you can use your computer if you are more comfortable with that. Just create a journaling folder and give it a name that you can find when you need it.

Not a journaler? Let me remind you what Paul says in 2 Corinthians 3:3. "You show you are a letter from Christ . . . written not with ink but with the spirit of the living god, not on tablets of stone but on tablets of human hearts."

You are journaling. People are reading the message in your life's journal. Make sure what they read on every page points them to the Father.

FELLOWSHIP

All the things we've mentiioned are enhanced by your relationships with other believers. Though your relationship with God is a personal thing, the growth you experience can be enhanced and magnified by interacting with the body of Christ. When you have opportunity to fellowship with others, you are built up and made more effective in ministry.

Service to others also promotes personal growth. Giving of yourself gives you the opportunity to follow Jesus' example. When you find yourself in situations out of your comfort zone, you are able to stretch through total dependency on God. Flexing your spiritual muscles brings growth and strengthening.

Many writers tend to be introverts and avoid situations where there are lots of people. If you are an introvert, give yourself a push every once in a while and join a crowd of Christian brothers and sisters.

No matter what method of encouraging growth seems most comfortable to you, it is important to include each one in your quest for a wonderful relationship with God. As a writer, it is important that you continuously refill the source of love, joy, and fulfillment within you. You don't want your readers to have any question as to whether your glass is half full or half empty. You want them to read your writing and say, "Now there's a writer overflowing with the Spirit of God!"

THE MISSIONARY IN YOU

1. Do you think the word *spiritual* describes you? Why or why not?

2. What is the most important relationship in your life? Really think about your answer. Most of us know the answer should be your relationship with God, but do we live in a way that shows that is true?

3. What is your favorite place to worship?

4. Do you look at the world through eyes of faith? Or are you often tempted to look at things from a worldly perspective?

THE WRITER IN YOU

1. How does your personal Bible study affect what you write for others to read?

2. Prayer is an important part of the spirituality of a writer. Can you think of a time when you heard God give you direction about your writing?

3. Do you believe you are a writer on mission? Or are you just trying this writing thing out?

4. If you answered yes to question three, what is your mission? How did you hear God's call to write?

A WRITER'S PRAYER

Dear Father, Thank You for calling me to be a writer. What an honor to be Your messenger. I want to draw near to You so that I can overflow to the pages of my writing. There are millions of people in the world who need to know about You. I know I can't travel thousands of miles to tell them, but my books and articles can. Put wings to my words and send them to whoever needs to know about You. I love You and thank You for loving me so much. Amen.

Scripture Study: the Biblical Basis of a Writer on Mission

WRITING FROM THE WORD—AN ESSENTIAL STAGE OF WRITING FOR CHRIST

All Scripture is God-breathed and is useful for teaching, rebuking, correcting and training in righteousness, so that the man of God may be thoroughly equipped for every good work.

2 TIMOTHY 3:16–17

A big dilemma faced Patricia. She had to make a decision immediately. She had prayed, but had no clear direction from God. That day she prayed, "Lord, I must have Your answer. I need it now!" Then she opened her daily devotional reading and found these words: "In the time of my favor I will answer you" (Isaiah 49:8).

Taken aback, she just said, "Yes, sir."

In two days He gave her a miracle in which she didn't have to make a decision. He had already worked out the dilemma.

Jenna felt bored in a ministry that seemed stagnant. She opened her Bible and read: "Enlarge the place of your tent, stretch your tent curtains wide; do not hold back; lengthen your cords, strengthen your stakes" (Isaiah 54:2). She suggested the ministry remodel their building and begin several innovations to meet people's needs, and the ministry grew instantly.

In 1999 millions of people feared Y2K (year 2000). Experts predicted a huge computer system crash and worldwide economic disaster. Blakely had made several business decisions, but others around her still feared for the future. Just before January 1, 2000, she herself began to fear; she was afraid of disgrace if her plans failed. That week she listened as a conference leader read, "Because the sovereign Lord helps me, I will not be disgraced. Therefore I will set my face like flint; and I know I will not be disgraced."

After a broken engagement, Kensley went to a Bible study for comfort. Her teacher read, "I know your deeds. See, I have placed before you an open door and no man can shut it" (Revelation 3:8 KJV). Though those words were meant for the church at Sardis 2,000 years before, they spoke directly to Kensley. She says, "I knew God would bring me new opportunities and joy, and He did."

How many times have you found spiritual wisdom in certain Bible passages that seemed to answer your imminent questions at a certain time? As a Christian writer, you facilitate the joining of *spirit to Spirit* through Bible study.

SCRIPTURE STUDY OF A WRITER ON MISSION

Scripture study is part of discipleship in every Christian's life. For you to be the special writer on mission God intends you to be, you immerse yourself daily into the "abiding" John 15 speaks of, when Jesus says, "Abide in Me." Your spirit yearns for Him and finds Him in His Holy Scriptures. However, your curiosity also leads to another yearning: the joy of reading everything from dictionaries to literary journals to labels on tomato juice cans! Though God's Word is foundational and life-giving, a writer needs not only Scripture study, but also a study of other sources as well because a study of *life* is necessary to be a good writer.

I've heard many writers say they read more than they write. Most writers will diagnose their voracious reading habits as the identifying mark of a writer. In short, *writers are readers.* They avidly glean words and phrases from various sources. For many years I've faithfully read the *New Yorker* magazine. When Christian friends ask why I subscribe to this flagrantly secular magazine, I reply that it feeds my need to read great writing. I crave that exercise as a jump start for my brain.

What other kinds of writing does a writer on mission need? Good denominational lessons you trust, commentaries on the Scriptures, concordances, traditional and nontraditional ministry news, devotional books, newspaper accounts of up-to-date social issues affecting your community, autobiographies of Christian saints, and stories by authors who write excellent scriptural applications to life. Each of these makes you, the writer, an eclectic Christian and writer in training. And that training lasts till the end of your life.

If you live in the area known as Western civilization, certain stories in the Christian Bible are foundational for life. Allusions like "The British Empire was Goliath"; "You escaped the lion's den!"; "He buried his talent"; or "Keep your lamps burning" take on new meaning as a common culture understands the archetypal images of the Bible in our written and spoken word. Even words like *exodus* or *exile*, *Bathsheba* or *Jezebel* carry a special cultural meaning among learned people in Western civilization. Part of our education is that we understand "the widow's mite" does not describe an insect owned by a woman whose husband died.

No one worth his salt in the techniques of writing in the West can survive without a basic knowledge of the Ten Commandments or other classics in the Holy Scriptures. The Bible is foundational to many figures, stories, and literature courses in the Western literary world. Though the world is changing, it would be advantageous for today's writer to study carefully all parts of the Bible and master the techniques of the biblical writers to determine what they have to say to today's Christian writers. The parallelism in their poetry, the simplicity of balance in the psalms, and the precepts of storytelling found in allegories and parables are classics a religious writer today can cherish.

No doubt the Christian era from A.D. 100 through the twentieth century has diminished from some of its past grandeur. Queens and kings no longer dictate that their kingdoms must be Catholic, or Protestant—or even Christian, as Theodosius I did (February 27, A.D. 380). A few segments of Americans today are alarmed at the rise of other world religions. However, we have never had such opportunities as Christian writers to strengthen the power of the Word around the world. Electronic submissions, international dependence on economic symbiosis, and worldwide instant communication make the option to be a Christian writer an exciting path.

As an author, what are the basics to consider as you hone your writing techniques and sharpen your talent as God leads you? Research will include word study. Most Scriptures come from Hebrew (Old Testament) and Greek (New Testament) translations; therefore, a language exploration can uncover remarkable nuances of meaning. Through God's Spirit in His living Word, Jeremiah is able to reach across the centuries to tell you what God said to Him: "I will show you great and unsearchable things you do not know" (Jeremiah 33:3). Browsing through translations and keying in Christian words on your computer, you will recognize secrets you need to know. Your work comes alive as you discover new hidden meanings behind the Bible translations you read. In addition to a Hebrew/Greek/English equivalency book, study resource books with evangelistic materials based on Scriptures.

Suppose you want to write a nonfiction magazine article based on a specific topic. You choose to base most of the article on your own life experience: how to raise teenagers, since you have three teens at home, or how to overcome the depression of Parkinson's disease, since you have it. If you are writing fiction, you still find that the major characters evolve from your or your friends' experiences.

Success comes to both non-fictional and fictional work based solidly on Scripture, and is quickly recognized as shoddy work if it is not well investigated, reliable, and doctrinally correct.

> INVESTIGATION
> *Festus said to King Agrippa and his court:*
> *"I brought him [Paul] before all of you . . . so that as a result of this investigation I may have something to write"*
> (ACTS 25:26).
>
> *Help me, Lord, to investigate carefully so I will have something to write.*

MISSIONS

As a serious Christian writer, you probably already focus on Scripture study as a tool for reaching lost, sick, and hurting people. You know you can engage in evangelism and ministry as you serve God through your writing. Today may be the day God calls you to show others how to use Scriptures in pamphlets, magazine articles, handout sheets, or other materials. For instance, you may decide to write materials for your own denomination or nondenominational organizations who publish weekly Bible studies, curriculum, and witnessing leaflets. (See chaps. 6 and 7 for other ideas on writing as a ministry.) Parachurch companies and nondenominational organizations write books and manuals for support groups or fund-raising leaflets for nonprofit organizations.

Pray, asking God to show you a specific writing assignment. For example, you may feel led to write witnessing leaflets based directly on Scripture. Think of the steps in leading someone to ask Jesus into his or her heart. Research the topic by reading a few witnessing leaflets found online, in a Christian bookstore, or on a rack in a church hallway. Then begin writing an original, step-by-step process of becoming a Christian. Ask a doctrinal reader (clergy or seminary professor) to proofread your work, and send it, with a cover letter, to Christian publishers.

If you are clergy or a seminary professor, consider giant steps you can take to serve the Lord through your Scripture study. Begin recording your classes, homilies, sermons, and even elegies, to educate others as you share your knowledge of the Holy Scriptures. Later ask a secretary or a good typist to help transcribe these words for duplication. If you can, take time to key in the words yourself, asking only three others to join you in the room: the Father, the Son, and the Holy Spirit. If you have no advanced degrees or special Bible school training in a seminary or anywhere else, don't think you can ignore God's call to serve Him through writing Scripture studies. Share your wisdom. Think what you can record and duplicate. Start a collection of Bible passages you want to include. Gather illustrations and famous quotes to accompany the Scriptures.

A word of caution, however, if you are transcribing your sermons and other spoken messages. Very few spoken messages can be transcribed and printed as transcribed. It takes work to create a printed piece from spoken words. Don't take the obviously easier way out. Work on your material and create an effective written companion piece to your talks and sermons.

Another path to evangelism is writing Christian take-home papers. Think of this: every child or teen in every Sunday School takes home a handout about a Scripture verse, a catchy saying, a hands-on puzzle, or artwork from church. Someone has to write every handout. Why not you? Some churches use resource kits as illustrations for Bible study. *Your* words can change a boring Bible study to a life-changing Bible study.

You can change the world through your words. The Internet is a tool to change your dynamic words about a certain verse into vast avenues to reach lost, sick, and hurting people. The farthest point on the globe is within your grasp. Every day hundreds of people stand in line in the desert waiting to enter a tent with a few laptops they may use to communicate. Even in the most remote spot, people are learning about Christianity because the Word has power to reach them. Satellites and cyberspace create *immediate* communication. God has enabled you to live in a generation who could actually see Jesus instantly when He returns in the air! All at one time, from any point on earth, in an instant, we can look above Jerusalem into the sky and see what happens moment by moment!

[M] SECRETS

Sometimes your life's in a state of arrested spiritual development. If you've felt dry and flat on a spiritual plateau, go to God's Word. Once you know Jesus, the Word, and are sure you have a salvation experience (either in an aha moment or over time as He has nudged you closer to His heart), He wants you to draw nearer to Him daily. Through Scripture study, He reveals deep secrets hidden in His Word. New Testament writers called this a mystery. In Colossians 1:25–27, Paul says God has given him a

> *"commission to present to you the Word of God in all its fullness—the mystery that has been kept hidden for ages and generations, but is now disclosed to the saints. To them God has chosen to make known among the Gentiles the glorious riches of this mystery, which is Christ in you, the hope of glory."*

Paul wrote to the church in Colossae, a bustling commercial city. Think of a city near you that needs to know the *mystery* of Christ. It's a secret hidden in His Word that citizens haven't discovered before. Paul says you're a saint if you are a Christian.

God commissions us because the Word has been disclosed to the church. As Paul presented it to the church in Colossae, they're vicariously presenting it to us through the written word! God uses you and me to share deep secrets from His Word to our hearts, from our hearts to every stranger in the masses within a city—or a thousand cities. You can't possibly do that by yourself, but you do it easily by writing something of excellent quality that proclaims Jesus to others. Paul tells it like it is: you tell all the people you can influence about the glorious riches of this mystery: Christ in you—*you* are the hope of glory!

As you write, how can you totally explain truth: that Christ resides in you? You can't. It's an unexplainable personal relationship. But you can accept it on faith as you share Him, and in doing so, your words can become the hope of glory for the waiting world.

Look what Paul says about our methods: "We proclaim him, admonishing and teaching everyone with all wisdom, so that we may present everyone perfect in Christ. To this end I labor, struggling with all his energy, which so powerfully works in me" (Colossians 1:28–29). First, Paul tells you he *proclaims*. Through your words you will also proclaim God's truth. Paul also says he *admonishes*, or warns them seriously. Sometimes you may have to get serious with readers to get their attention! Then he says he *teaches*. He tells everything he knows in a clear, concise manner.

How does Paul teach? He says *with all wisdom*. Like Paul, you simply share everything you've learned through Scripture study and life experience, until your well overflows with the wisdom only God can bring. Now look at the end of this sentence in Paul's words above (v. 28). Who is Paul's audience? He says it's *everyone*. (Don't define your audience as "everyone" in a proposal to an acquisitions editor at a publishing house, but you do need to decide on a target audience!) *Who's* going to read your writing? Is your audience your children or grandchildren? Is it your local church congregation?

How about unchurched people? Paul wants the whole world to know the gospel. It's remarkable that within a few centuries, his letters were spread all over the known world. They were even reprinted 2,000 years later!

Why does Paul proclaim, admonish, and teach? He says he aims to "present everyone perfect in Christ." You can help your readers see they are sinners and can be perfect only when Christ cleans them up. This is the core truth of the gospel for everybody on earth. Paul says in Ephesians 1, "He chose us in him before the creation of the world to be holy and blameless in his sight." *What's* Paul's aim? "Perfecting" people by introducing them to Christ, the Perfect One, who'll save them from punishment caused by sin. They'll be holy and blameless in His sight! Since Paul identifies everyone as his audience, his aim includes you, the writer, and all your readers. With everyone focused on this truth, our *mission of world evangelization is obvious.* We write to tell everyone within our influence about Jesus as a personal Savior.

Like any writer, Paul finds proclaiming, admonishing, and teaching with wisdom a hard task. He clearly says he labors and struggles. You probably also struggle as you proclaim the gospel through your words. He's looking for the end result, telling you how to be successful: through Jesus' energy, which works *powerfully* in you as well as Paul. Is it going to be easy for you to write? No. It will continue to be a labor, a struggle. But you'll be able to proclaim Him, getting your readers' attention to teach them what the Scriptures say—with more wisdom and energy than you ever had before—because of the Spirit of Jesus that works in you *powerfully!*

D DISCOVERIES

When did you first memorize a Bible verse? As a writer, you may be surprised at the number of verses that pop into your mind when you need them. Whether you memorized these passages in Sunday

School, Christian high school training, seminary experience, a church discipleship study, or from a member of your family, these words from the past can change the future.

In a supernatural way, Bible study changes hearts. Before you write to help others, you need to discover the mystery of Bible study as it changes your heart. Paul says to the church at Colossae: "Let the word of Christ dwell in you richly as you teach and admonish one another with all wisdom, and as you sing psalms, hymns and spiritual songs with gratitude in your hearts to God" (Colossians 3:16). Before you write, spend time reading Scriptures and singing scriptural passages you recall. Praise God with heartfelt gratitude. As Paul says in another verse (3:17), pray in Jesus' name and then write in Jesus' name. "Do it all in the name of the Lord Jesus, giving thanks to God the Father through him."

Proverbs 16:24 says, "Pleasant words are a honeycomb, sweet to the soul and healing to the bones." Whatever form your Bible study takes, its aim should be to sweeten the soul and heal the bones of those who are hurting physically and spiritually. Your mission, if you decide to accept it, is to bring a sweet spirit to the reader and heal a sin-sick soul as God moves through your words. As you write the best study possible, seek the proper form to deliver the appropriate message for your reader. Bible study opportunities don't always take the form of a book. Think large and small. Will your work be a ten-volume Bible concordance with an annotated study? Will it be a compilation book with other writers' contributions? Will it be a workbook? What are possibilities for an angle or slant to your Bible study?

Wayne Harvey just completed a Bible study by compiling the idioms of the Bible, a scholarly work (*Raising Cain and Other Idioms*). Will your book be scholarly? Humorous? Reader friendly? Written in today's teen lingo? You choose the option.

Magazine articles are read by millions worldwide every day. Compare that figure with the number of books on the market. Most Christian books today will sell less than 1,000 copies. Of course, it's possible your Bible study may be a best seller; but if you want to influence more people for Christ, magazine articles are the forerunners right now.

Think of articles in daily newspapers, which touch millions daily. Could your short Bible study become a syndicated phenomenon among Christian readers causing newspapers everywhere to read your fascinating "Bible Moments" (or whatever God allows your column to be called)?

On the other hand, think of a small giftbook that doesn't sell as many copies but will be passed from generation to generation, friend to friend, over many decades. Does that impact sound like something God may do with your writing?

Popularity is growing dynamically with ezines and online books and articles. Web sites with blogs, online interviews, and texted or spoken Bible studies are exploding. Explore Web sites with call-in spots for "experts" in all topics, especially in Scripture interpretations for daily life.

STORYING

One essential feature for every nonfiction book is storytelling. A story is a useful element of any Bible study. It can be used as a practical example for your family to read, a humorous anecdote to hook the average reader, or a warm-and-fuzzy avenue to a stranger's heart. As you form a good story, picture your grandchild enjoying it.

Standard form. Most stories follow this outline: *setting* (time, place, characters), a *point of tension* (the beginning of a plot), followed by *rising action* elevating tension to a high point. The *climax* occurs at the highest point of action, sometimes called the point of no return, when the reader can't go back. (Someone dies, leaves, or moves to a different perspective, never to revert to the previous one.)

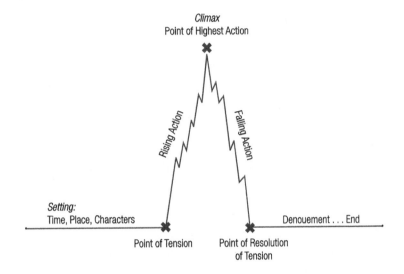

Following the story's climax, *falling action*, usually shorter than rising action, ends in *denouement*, resolving the tension or initial problem. After all is resolved, the end is humorous, happy, or sometimes sad. The characters may have learned something, entertained the audience/readers, or grown in truth to be sadder but wiser.

Whoever is reading your story, it can be used in the following ways:

Introductions. A story serves as a hook that captures the reader from the beginning. It can be Christian fiction or a true story related to Bible study that takes place in a certain setting, but it must be believable. It needs to shock, excite, anger, or surprise your audience to get their attention. A carefully chosen story compels the reader to read further.

Remember your favorite stories from your childhood? Recall those your Boy Scout leaders or family told around a campfire or at bedtime. They usually included a compelling introduction, followed by lots of rising and falling action. A good tale is the stuff from which life is made. It carries archetypes of life that resonate within our souls.

Point illustrations. Your chapters come alive if you use quick stories to illustrate: insert a short story following point A, another following point B, and a third following point C, etc., when appropriate, to explain and satisfy your readers. Every point doesn't need a story, but when a good one comes to mind to illustrate the point, use it.

Chapter endings. Another useful way to use a story comes at chapter endings. A heartwarming story can make the reader say, "Ah . . . now the Bible study is over." It can resolve the tension or challenges in a study. Every brief story doesn't have to contain all these elaborate parts, but you can see this story pattern even in a short vignette that concludes a Bible study chapter. Even a brief story can lead your reader to think you're a genius because of your endings!

Personal application. True stories supply inspiration for readers to apply the study passage to their lives. List your own stories; then interview others to get their true stories and file them away in your "Fodder" file under Bible study categories. For example, recall a humorous story under the point "Mistakes Christians Make That Embarrass Us," or recall a poignant story under "When We Survive a Broken Heart." Not all parts of Bible study chapters require a story, but a good study chapter may provide one or two.

Choose some of the suggestions in this chapter and the next, writing from God's Word, an essential stage in writing for Christ.

THE MISSIONARY IN YOU

1. In which segments of your life have you met people you might influence through God's Word?
2. What traits do you have that will help you admonish, proclaim, and teach others about Jesus?
3. Which secrets of the gospel have you discovered that you could share with others?
4. Look back at the Scripture verse at the beginning of this chapter. Thank God for all the times He has breathed life into His Word that encouraged or corrected you when you needed it. Name people whose lives have been changed through Scriptures.

THE WRITER IN YOU

1. For which area of writing do you have a passion? To be a better writer, in which areas do you need training?
2. Are you a storyteller? How will you use stories in your Scripture studies?
3. Which Scripture passages have been foundational in your life? How can you use these to focus on becoming a writer on mission?
4. Proverbs 12:25 says, "An anxious heart weighs a man down, but a kind word cheers him up." Are your words anxious or kind? Do they cheer up someone else's life?

A WRITERS PRAYER

Eternal Writer, I pray for Your discernment today as I write to help others discover hidden secrets in Your Word. As I proclaim, admonish, and teach what You have taught me, please help me state exact truth and warm the heart of my target audience. With Your sovereign wisdom, may I write pleasant words to sweeten the souls and heal the bones of those who are hurting. Give me word power to usher Your Spirit into the spirit of every reader. In Jesus' name, amen.

The Basics of Writing a Scripture Study

FROM THE WORD—HOW TO USE YOUR WRITING AS A STUDY GUIDE

All this I have in writing from the hand of the Lord upon me, and he gave me understanding in all the details of the plan.

1 CHRONICLES 28:19

"I've made things right with God." Jack told his fellow writers he had taken the first step, establishing the right spiritual attitude. He had looked at a few ideas, scanned several resources, assumed an attitude of prayer, and was ready to work closely with God as he wrote. After you look into your heart and make contact with God, you are ready to start writing.

Whether writing your life story for your grandchildren or writing large volumes for more formal publication, you need to present Scriptures for your reader. Your son or daughter, and grandson or granddaughter, at some time in their lives, will savor your favorite verses as they learn how you depended on them across the years. Your stories about special verses will be a blessing to all your descendants. In a more formal work, hundreds may use your explanation of the Holy Scriptures and use them to encourage thousands of others through the years. Stories about your favorite Scriptures will be found not only on the pages of a book like this but also in electronic media, where your words will be saved for centuries.

ORGANIZATION

Before you begin, think about how your written Bible study would compare with others you studied as a child, a teen, or an adult. Think of Sunday School or discipleship classes you took and the characteristics of the Bible studies that became your favorites. Then pray for God's guidance as you write. Discern how He seems to be nudging you to develop your Bible study for others. Let's say, for instance, that you are writing a Bible study book for a small-group study. If you have accepted the challenge to write, whether it is a book, a magazine article, or a short memoir, a good Bible study should include the following.

PRESENTATION

The first essential for Bible study is a presentation of the Scripture verses. As you browse through other current Bible studies, you'll find some include the Scripture itself, highlighted in a tool-lined box or surrounded by artwork. In other studies instructions tell the reader to read the Scripture passage, but the text does not include it. The reader can then choose his or her favorite version of the Bible. Both methods have advantages. If the Scripture is included in your Bible study book, the reader has everything in one place for easy reading. If a group is studying together, they all have the same translation and each focuses easily on the same place in the text.

On the contrary, sometimes readers may not enjoy the version you've included in your book. Some may insist on the King James Version, for example, and others may judge that version hard to read and yearn for a contemporary translation. If they choose the Bible version themselves, everyone is content. You present the Bible study without quoting word-for-word so readers will be able to use their own Bibles with familiar translations. In the presentation of material, you may briefly mention background information with setting and situation, followed by the main points of the Scripture.

EXPLICATION

Following the presentation of Scripture verses, give an explication, or explanation, of the verses, providing the basics of the subject matter in the passage. To define unfamiliar words, you may use dictionary definitions, commentary references, concordance information, or your ideas as an authority on the passage. In Galatians 1, for example, you may define or clarify the usage of *apostle* (vv. 1, 17, 19), *grace* (vv. 3, 16), *Judaism* (vv. 13, 14), and *Gentiles* (v. 16). As God leads you, break down certain elements of the Scripture for close scrutiny, and explain what you find in a concordance or online about these words. For instance, take a one-sentence verse, such as Galatians 1:20. "I assure you before God that what I am writing is no lie." This may be a verse you've never looked at closely before. Find dictionary definitions of the main words: *assure, God, writing,* and *lie.* Check a concordance for alternate meanings to these words. Then select the major parts of the sentence to decipher the meaning. If you know how, diagram sentences in your mind until you pick apart the construction and clarify the author's meaning. In this sentence, what exactly is no lie? If the word *what* is the subject of the verb *is,* then *what I am writing* is no lie. Paul is swearing the words he has authored are truthful. Continue to break down parts of the Scripture passage until you've uncovered the truth God leads you to explain.

ELABORATION

This segment adds more "meat" to your chapter. Using key translations of Hebrew words in the Old Testament or Greek words in the New Testament, you may uncover remarkable meanings. As you reveal these special word usages for your readers, the verses of Scripture may enlighten them and change their lives. You may compare the meaning of certain words in Bible days to the meaning today. Your elaboration may feature comparisons of key relationships, the influence of culture, or suggestions of related passages that embellish the meaning or the content. In Galatians 1:20 in the paragraph above, you could identify the writer, Paul, and tell your reader how his Jewish culture was different from the secular culture of the Gentiles in Galatia. Why would they think his words would be a lie? Explain why you think he felt it necessary to assure them he was telling the truth *before God*. Describe the serious nature of a solemn oath before God to a Jewish man like Paul. You may provide questions to consider, list extended facts from your research, or add a sidebar containing cultural habits of first-century Jewish society to help readers understand. This segment allows you to use your best flair for writing inspirational prose.

APPLICATION

The ending segment brings readers full circle from approaching the Scripture in the presentation to applying it to their own situations in the application. This ending segment may include questions about a reader's spiritual life, further study passages for follow-up, suggestions for behavior modification in the reader's life, the application of family values seen in this passage, or other lifestyle applications.

Remember, the application is your opportunity to touch the heart of your reader.

> *"The application is your opportunity to touch the heart of your reader."*

HANDLING SCRIPTURE AS A WRITER ON MISSION

In any leadership book such as this, you are basically training trainers, hoping your readers will understand certain passages of Scripture and share their knowledge with others. Handling God's Holy Scripture and interpreting it for others who will learn from your book is a delicate matter. Men and women throughout history have been burned at the stake or beheaded for meddling with God's Word! Though times have changed, respect for His Holy Word is still a reverent matter. The importance of doctrinal accuracy and careful verification is vital to the integrity of the gospel. Remember, whether you are writing for your grandchild or for seminary students, use caution as you explain Bible passages. Pray that God will guide you as you demonstrate reverence for His Word.

Many writers experience a phenomenon called *writer's block* and just can't get started. Sometimes a call to writing, as part of God's plan for the world, is overwhelming. The privilege of writing *for Him* and *with Him* is inspiring, yet sometimes intimidating. If you feel you have writer's block and simply can't start writing, remember, there are two cures for writer's block. First, don't start. Begin in the middle. Write what you know about one concept, illustration, or character in the work. Write whatever made you think you could write in the first place—whether it is a Christian magazine article, a children's picture book, your spiritual autobiography, or a scholarly book on apologetics. Once you write the middle, then go back and write an introduction and a conclusion. You don't have to start with an introduction or follow a preconceived outline. The work will grow a life of its own and change several times before you finish it anyway. Remember, you begin in a fluid state. Relax, write what you know, and enjoy the process.

Second, another way to ease writer's block is to face that writer's block is nonexistent. It is simply a hesitation of a perfectionist. You may have writer's block because you are afraid what you write next will be imperfect. Pride in your perfection is sin. Forget all other reasons for writer's block. Follow these four logical steps as you talk with God.

1. OK. I'm a perfectionist.

2. Lord, I'm acknowledging I'm imperfect. You know it. I know it.

3. I'm going to write something imperfectly today. I'll wander, I'll key in nonsense, and I'll make mistakes.

4. I'm beginning my prewriting now, using stream-of-consciousness technique: whatever pops into my mind is going down. Now!

L LOOK

Before they begin writing, some writers observe a time in which they take a look at their subject matter or get involved with their topic. This is the *preliminary research* stage of writing. A good way to begin to write a Bible study is to set aside a certain time every day for your personal Bible study. Without reinventing the wheel, *look* at what's already in print. Select a good study by asking friends, looking online, or digging in old study books from your family or church. Don't worry if you have little time to research. Be brief. Fifteen minutes a day for four days is as good as an hour-long research session. Scan examples of well-done commentary on good Scripture passages or a training book on study methods. Take notes. Save a list of your favorite passages. Create a "Fodder" file of ideas to apply later as theme illustrations. Use this time to ask God to help you as you write.

N NOOK

No, this is not an electronic device for reading books. This is the time-honored stage of *prewriting*. A *nook* is your favorite place to snuggle down and write the beginning drafts of an article or a book: your adjustable desk chair with a computer in front of you, a comfortable recliner with a laptop, or propped up in bed in your pajamas with six pillows and a legal pad.

One of the most important principles for a Bible study writer is to know your best techniques for writing about God's Holy Word. Prewriting is an important phase in the process. Jot down a temporary outline as you go. Don't fuss over details or stop to correct every typo. Just nook or cocoon for a while, getting down the broad ideas God gives you. This traditional prewriting is a time to experiment with your style. Assume you are entering your own niche, your little nook-zone for writing. If God directs you toward an aim for the ending of the work, set that down, as clearly as you can, in a prominent place you can view from time to time as you write. For example, God might nudge you to focus on telling one person at a time about Jesus. That missions focus is important. Some writers tape goals on the wall behind their computer monitors; others write a central focus in large letters on the cover of their notebooks propped up on the back of their desks. Whatever works for you, do some deep thinking and praying during the prewriting stage. Write something, even if you know it's wrong . . . for now. Each writer has his or her own pace in a special nook. Get in your zone and write!

H HOOK

This is the *heart-central* stage of writing, the point at which you buckle down and do the most difficult major writing: you transform your research and prewriting into a rough draft. It includes the organization of your Bible study content: presentation, explication, elaboration, and application. You will rethink your starting point: begin each chapter or segment with a *hook*: a shocking fact, a story, or an introduction to hook your reader. Then you start the magical process of hooking your ideas together in an orderly way, using transitions between segments. If you're a global thinker writing a book, you can see the title of every chapter and set a goal for each. If you're a detail thinker, you can get lost researching facts and forget where you are in the broad scheme of things. Whereas you didn't worry about details or order in the prewriting stage, now is the time to worry about significant details. Make sure your segments tie together in a smooth flow. Finish a first draft of the piece. If you are working on a long piece, such as a book, finish a first draft of each chapter and then compile them into a first draft of the entire book.

Writing a rough draft is also a time to experiment with your style. Have fun as you add new phrases, try a flowery description, or decide to cut out superfluous words and cut to the chase. If you want a following of readers, you want to establish a style they love to read. Get down to earth, think of your major focus and your audience, and finish that first draft.

B BOOK

This is the *polishing* stage of writing—where you make it into a real *book*. Make sure you use only one space after periods at the end of sentences. Leave no orphans at the end of paragraphs or pages and widows at the beginnings of pages. (Cutting one unnecessary word somewhere in the paragraph will move the other words up or down to join the rest of the paragraph.) Eliminate all unnecessary words throughout the manuscript. This tightening saves money overall from wasted paper and digital space, so editors love it! Double-check any misspellings the computer has missed (for instance, *their* instead of *there* or *it's* instead of *its*.) Check for weird spacing or a change of font related to automatic computer changes.

Stick to your mission for writing this piece. If you are writing for your family or for unchurched people in Africa, ask yourself if it fulfilled its purpose. Change wording to soften your diction if the words could hurt a reader. Use other names if a family member is sensitive about any family matter. Be sure you have used proper social etiquette by not insulting any friend or revealing a personal issue that invades privacy. Remember, what you write is permanent. It will remain long after your death and can survive in cyberspace forever.

Do a final proofread (or ask several friends or an editor to proofread for you). Then do a final edit, checking for other things in addition to typos, grammar errors, and misused words. Go through a final massacre of unnecessary words to trim your manuscript to a *tight write* before you print it.

Writers of the Bible have much to say to a writer today, but you can ruin the thoughts of these God-inspired men if you fail to quote them accurately. Double-check your quotations as a last preparation for publication. If you are quoting a Bible passage word for word, decide first on the translation you'll use. Then learn the proper way to cite the passage: Use present tense. Do not italicize, underline, or boldface the passage. Use quotation marks to set off a quotation that is in your running text.

> If your quotation is long (more than 100 words or longer than six to eight lines), indent the entire passage on the left. Some publishers ask you to indent on the right as well. You will also see the type size of a block quotation reduced by one point size. For instance, if your manuscript is written in 12-point font size, reduce the block quotes to 11-point font size. Some of these things are decided by the publisher's designer, so be sure to ask your publisher for a style sheet before you begin your work. (This paragraph is not a quote but is an example of possible block quotation form.)

VERIFICATION

Nothing is more important than your verification of sources in interpreting God's Word. Even if your work will be read only by family, you'll want to set a good example before them and honor God's Word through proper verification. Make your writing the best it can be. Always obtain permission to use a quote that is copyrighted and state you are using it with permission granted.

Keep a copy of the following: the cover page of the book from which you took the quote, the inside cover, including the copyright information and ISBN number, and the page (including the page number) of the original quote. If you use a professional publisher for your written material, code your verification pages with A, B, C, etc.

Example: Ellison verification A: p. 321, paragraph 4, lines 3–4.

Then mark the page where you used the quote in your book or article manuscript: "Verification A."

You may write the above line (1) in the margin of the hard copy, if you turn one in; (2) on an electronic "review" page recorded in an emailed document; or (3) on a disk or even a thumb drive sent to your publisher.

Keep verification page(s) and letters of permission,, and attach a copy at the back of the final manuscript for the publisher's records, or provide scans by email. Be sure to keep another copy of both the manuscript and the verification pages, clearly marked, for your records. Double-check to be sure each verification is carefully marked to match the appropriate page of your manuscript.

 CITATIONS

Don't use footnotes. Use endnotes, if requested by your publisher. Otherwise, just place the quoted material in the body of your paragraph and use a citation, without stopping to cite completely.

This is an example of a citation: (John 3:16).

As in any work, you will place quotation marks before and after a passage of Scripture. However, note the placing of quotation marks and the ending periods below:

Paul says, "I can do everything through him who gives me strength" (Philippians 4:13).

If your quote is from the Bible translation used throughout the book, you do not need to cite the translation after each entry.

- Commas and periods come inside the quotation marks, unless followed by a citation.
- Colons (:) and semicolons (;) come outside quotation marks.
- Exclamation points (!) and question marks (?) may come inside or outside the quotation marks, depending on the way they are used. (Example: Use the question mark inside, if the quote is a question.)

1. Paul says, "I can do everything" (Philippians 4:13).
2. Paul says, "I can do all things through Christ, who gives me strength" (Philippians 4:13 KJV).
3. Paul says in Philippians, "I can do everything."
4. Paul says in Philippians, "I can do everything," and he did.
5. Paul says in Philippians, "I can do everything": preach, teach, admonish, and praise God!
6. Paul says in Philippians, "I can do everything"; he did everything he possibly could.
7. Paul says in Philippians, "Can I do everything?"
8. Does Paul say in Philippians, "I can do everything"?
9. Paul says with a shout, "I can do everything!"
10. Wow! I just know Paul quietly whispers, "I can do everything"!

Various publishers use style sheets (not just one sheet, but a short booklet) that will usually suggest you use a preferred stylebook as a reference. For example, many Christian publishers today choose *The Chicago Manual of Style*, a large book with comprehensive directions for writers. Do exactly as your publisher suggests: follow the stylebook (in the preferred edition) and the publisher's style sheets. Also adhere to the publisher's preferred dictionary source.

 COOK

This is the *pause* stage of writing. After you have completed the manuscript and tended to final details, set it aside and let it *cook* for several days—the longer the better. Then figuratively take it out of the oven (off the shelf) and peruse it like an objective reader. Check to be sure you stuck to your mission: to do your part of God's evangelization of the world in your own corner of influence. Does your mission match your manuscript? Be sure you didn't lose focus of your major missions objective. Skim with fresh eyes to details one last time before you send it to the printer for publication.

 TOOK

This is the *follow-through* stage of writing. Make sure your *efforts took*. Double-check your form. Make sure your pages are numbered and properly identified. If your publisher wants numbers, insert them as headers or footers, don't place them in regular lines on the page. Remember, page numbers will be stripped and new ones added on the published work. Attach your document to an email. If your publisher or printer wants a hard copy or a disk of your work, take the manuscript to the post office or a mail service and send it.

May God give you the integrity and Spirit to interpret and write Bible studies for Him as He encourages you to be a writer on mission.

THE MISSIONARY IN YOU

1. How do you see your mission fulfilled during the application segment of writing from God's Word?

2. How can you ensure you'll write with integrity, reverence, and inspired words?

3. How do you avoid plagiarism?

4. Where is your favorite "nook" for writing?

THE WRITER IN YOU

1. Which stage of writing is easiest for you? (look, nook, hook, book, cook, took)

2. Which is more important, staying focused on your writing mission or learning more about the writing craft (grammar, spelling, other mechanics)?

3. How many days do you usually plan for your writing to "cook"? Is it hard to set it aside on a shelf for a long period so you can scan and edit it with fresh eyes?

4. What was the most important writer tip in this chapter?

A WRITER'S PRAYER

O God, I pray humbly because of Your Holy Word. Thank You for all the verses of blessing that encourage and strengthen me as a writer. May they always give me peace and power to stay focused on my Christian mission, and may I interpret Your Word accurately as a witness to those who don't know You. Help my words to flow freely as I write through Your process. Thank You for giving me the scriptural story of Jesus, who died for my sins, in whose name I pray, amen.

Worldview: A Pivotal Point of a Writer on Mission

WRITING THROUGH PERSPECTIVE—A PIVOTAL STAGE IN WRITING FOR CHRIST

Do not conform any longer to the pattern of this world, but be transformed by the renewing of your mind. Then you will be able to test and approve what God's will is—His good, pleasing and perfect will.

ROMANS 12:2

While driving home one night, Snow saw something in the road ahead. He stopped and found a young man zoned out on drugs, lying on the yellow line at the center of the road. He was wearing no shoes, shirt, or underwear—just a pair of jeans. His long, stringy hair hung matted together below his shoulders, and he had scratches on his shoulders and feet.

Snow quickly picked him up and found a safe place at his community's town hall for him to spend the night. The next morning he provided a bath, clean clothes, and a good meal. Over the hearty breakfast, Snow found out that the teenager, Johnny, from a distant state, had been hooked on drugs for two years but had reached rock bottom. For a few months, he had slipped into his parents' basement and slept on a coal pile, but that week they had found him and kicked him out. He had hitchhiked, begging for enough money to survive, until finally he arrived in our town and collapsed on the road. Some of Snow's friends who learned about Johnny's situation gave him clothes, secured a place for him to live, and got him into a rehabilitation clinic.

A few months later, Snow and his wife went to their usual weekly community Bible study. They had a good crowd, with a few new young adults.

If only Johnny could come to this Bible study every week, the wife thought, *it would make a difference in his life.* She planned to ask him to come with them after he got out of rehab. Snow walked over to welcome the young men, while she talked to another woman beside her. Later she glanced at the guy next to Snow. *How healthy and clean-cut he looks,* she thought. His short haircut made him even more handsome. *A nice young man too.*

In a moment, Snow motioned her to come over. He said, "Honey, do you remember the young man I found that night on Sloan Street?"

"Yes," she said, "Johnny. I was just thinking of him, wishing he could come to this Bible study every . . ."

"I want you to meet Johnny Smith," he said, beaming.

She was stunned. He was not the same guy Snow had found on the streets. . . . Couldn't be! She looked at him again.

It *was* Johnny! He shook her hand, thanking her for their help. He had changed completely, inside and out. He eagerly told them how God had shown him how to reach outside himself and help others less fortunate than he was. He had reconciled with his parents, and had a new job.

"He's going to help with the men's soup kitchen project next week!" Snow said.

From that moment, Johnny was rehabilitated. He had been to clinics to dry out before, but nothing had worked. This time, he said, something had happened to him. As part of a 12-step program at the Christian rehab facility, a staff member had led Him to invite Jesus into his heart. He was never the same. Someone gave him a Bible, and it enlarged His life's view and his lifestyle. "I have a new heart," he said." I care about the world."

Johnny had experienced a complete shift in his worldview.

WORLDVIEW OF A WRITER ON MISSION

Worldview is simply the filter through which we see the world. Christians see the world one way; Hindus, another. Atheists, still another way. When an atheist man finds Jesus as his Savior, his worldview explodes with new meaning, as he changes the filter through which he sees his children, his wife, and his community. God gives us many examples of people whose worldview changed in miraculous ways. One of the most dramatic is that of Saul of Tarsus, who, as a zealous Jewish rabbi, was seeking out people of the new heretical group called Christians, or people of the Way, and killing them. He watched as hundreds of Christian converts were stoned or fed to lions (Acts 7:59 to 8:1). Then one day his worldview changed dramatically. After obtaining letters of introduction from the high priest in Jerusalem, he headed for Damascus to find people of the Way and take his prisoners back to Jerusalem for punishment (Acts 9:1–2). After a flash of light from God hit him, he fell to his knees and heard Jesus ask, "Saul, Saul, Why do you persecute me?" (vv. 3–4). Saul rose up blind, but over the next few days God healed him and gave him a new name, Paul.

As most Christians know, the Apostle Paul made a 180-degree turnaround, becoming a zealous Christian evangelist. He quickly became an itinerant missionary and eventually the author of most of the New Testament epistles.

Most Christian writers have made that same 180-degree turnaround at some point in their lives. Because we've expanded our view of the world, we write so others can also make that change in their lives as they read God's Word in inspirational literature. Paul says to the church in Rome, "How beautiful are the feet of those who bring good news" (Romans 10:15). He was quoting Isaiah (52:7), who also said, "Those who bring good news, who proclaim peace, who bring good tidings, who proclaim salvation, who say to Zion, 'Your God reigns!'"

Wow! Does that description sound like you? Do you have a heart for bringing good news, the gospel, to others? God calls you to proclaim your worldview of peace and salvation, and to praise Him, as Paul did in Zion (Jerusalem). Paul not only praised God in the very town that was his headquarters for persecution of Christians, but he also praised God in many other places as he became the first Christian missionary to the *Gentile* as well as to the *Jewish* world.

Elizabeth Ford was interested in helping poor women near Fort Mill, South Carolina, who dug furniture, clothes, and even food from the dumpsters at the local trash dump. Elizabeth, along with others who cared, began a Christian Women's Job Corps® (CWJC®) in the area. For months CWJC mentors and trainers gave Christian hope to the women as they helped them work toward getting a job to support their children and get off government support. "We were giving a hand up, not a handout," she said. Then one day after months of training, Elizabeth and other CWJC council members went to see the women they had trained. To their surprise, they were not at home, but were down at the trash dump. Elizabeth feared the women had lost the hope they had shared, and the women had returned to depression and a victim-focused worldview. When they arrived at the dumpsters, Elizabeth and her team found the women had started a ministry to other women who had not yet been helped by CWJC and were digging in the trash to survive!

The miracle that took place in these women's hearts was a simple one that happens often when people become Christians. It was a change in worldview. They had stopped seeing the world through a victim mentality. After being mentored and trained for a change of lifestyle, they felt enabled, not only to earn a living for themselves and their children, but also to give out of their reserve to help others! They were philanthropists at the trash dump!

POINT OF VIEW

One factor writers on mission consider in their writing is point of view (POV). As you read the writing of other authors, you'll notice they write from one or several of these points of view:

Personal: When writing in personal point of view, the writer uses first-person pronouns: *I, me, my, mine, we, us, our,* and *ours.* In a novel personal POV looks like this: *I wandered across the dark moors that morning and thought about Sutlive walking with me when we visited Aunt Mary. I knew he cared about my position in life and I smiled at the thought of our friendship.*

In personal POV, the reader's stream of consciousness is inside the head of the person whose persona is speaking or thinking. Readers see through the eyes of the persona and think as that character does. They see other characters only as the persona sees them, and cannot know what's in the heads of other characters. They understand them only through the actions or appearance of others as the persona looks at them.

In nonfiction, personal POV is useful if you're writing a memoir or a personal story to use as a hook to introduce a chapter. Personal POV presents a warm style and is easy to read. Readers can sympathize and understand the main character.

Narrative: When writing in an objective narrative point of view, the writer uses third-person pronouns: *he, him, his, she, her, hers, it, its, they, them, their,* and *theirs.* An objective storyteller presents a narrative. In the short play *Our Town,* Thornton Wilder creates a stage-manager narrator who stands by a ladder telling the love story of Emily and George, teenagers in Grover's Corners. Since the stream of consciousness is inside the narrator's head, narrative POV is, of course, more objective than personal.

In an objective narrative POV, the writing looks like this: *Holding hands, the handsome young couple walks into the distance on the deserted island, looking toward the sunrise, which may provide a ship today.* You are perhaps standing in the background, far away from the main characters, as an objective narrator might describe the scene. Expecting a ship is a clue given by the narrator, but not a personal thought in the couple's minds.

Omniscient (*omni*: all; *scient*: knowing): When writing in omniscient point of view, the stream of consciousness can be anywhere. Readers can know what every character is thinking at a given time, or go across the country to a scene in another place, without being in anyone's mind. In Jack London's *The Call of the Wild,* the main character struggles to survive, finally freezing in the snow. After he dies, London reveals *what the dog is thinking* as he trots back to camp for supper! Omniscient POV is not respected by editors in the twenty-first century. It is confusing to readers and writers seldom use it.

Limited Omniscient: When writing in limited omniscient point of view, the reader feels as if he or she stands at the elbow of the main persona, or protagonist, where he or she can see everything others do, but knows everything from the personal thoughts of that one person and never telling the reader things the main persona, or protagonist, doesn't know. This is the most popular way to write fiction as we follow one character and see the world through his or her eyes. Limited omniscient POV looks like this: *She peered out the window at Ellen, but could not see what she was holding behind her back. . . . Was it a wallet or a book? Oh my best friend. Are you my friend or enemy?*

Alternating: When writing in an alternating POV, the writer sometimes surprises the reader by head-hopping from one person's head to another. One good example of this is the "Harry Potter" series, where we follow Harry most of the time, and suddenly we find we're inside another person's head in our stream of consciousness, flying through the air on a broom or slamming into a wall at a railway station.

Epistolary: When writing in an epistolary POV, the writer uses letters or documents to show the plot or display the hearts and passion of the characters. You may decide to use this POV if you have love letters or legal documents from your family and want to preserve the interesting story of your missionary ancestors in China for your descendants to read. You may also use key passages in the Pauline letters with little commentary if you want to tell unchurched people groups how God changed Saul's persecution worldview to that of an evangelist apostle. Use epistolary point of view if you're working on historical documents, such as the next batch of Dead Sea Scrolls, and want to share earthshaking news with the Christian world.

Second person: When writing in a second-person POV, the writer uses second-person pronouns: *you, your, yours,* and *yourself.* It's OK to write in the imperative mood, with commands. In most manuscripts you do not want to call attention to the author. However, if you're writing a manual or a how-to booklet/pamphlet of any kind, you'll find second-person point of view to be helpful. Writing genres that fall into this category are support group instructions, inspirational nonfiction based on tragic experience, manuals for caregivers or mentors, denominational scope and sequence books, Christian school curriculum, and children's books on how to encourage their friends. The reader knows you are giving him or her personal advice and accepts your instructional words. Though you want to avoid preachy language in 99 percent of your writing, a didactic style and second-person point of view can be helpful as you write in the imperative mood. For example: *Never allow the patient to fall out of bed. Secure the side bars and monitor his progress during the day. To be a blessing to the patient, a Christian caregiver can find many ways to cheer up the family. Smile. Tell a humorous story. Give a Bible verse on your business card.*

Bible writers often used second-person POV to write imperative sentences to encourage their readers. Paul says, "Do nothing out of selfish ambition. . . . Consider others better than yourselves" (Philippians 2:3). "Stand firm in the Lord, dear friends! . . . Rejoice in the Lord always. I will say it again: Rejoice" (4:1, 4)! The writer of Hebrews softens his style by using the first-person plural: "Let us throw off everything that hinders and the sin that so easily entangles, and let us run with perseverance. . . . Let us fix our eyes on Jesus. . . . Make every effort to live in peace with all men. . . . See to it that . . . no bitter root grows up to cause trouble. . . . See that no one is sexually immoral" (Hebrews 12:1–2, 14–16).

Mixing POVs: As a general rule, don't mix points of view. Avoid jolting your reader by head-hopping or jumping from one POV to another. If you feel you must tell your reader something the main persona does not know, then use one point of view in one chapter and another point of view in the next. You may feel compelled to use more than one point of view in the same chapter. Don't do this unless you make sure there's a clean break between scenes and you can begin a new POV in the next scene, usually in a different setting. After you have finished your work, check your POV to be sure your thoughts flow smoothly from one scene to another. (Do you recognize this paragraph as a didactic, second-person, imperative style? Did its preachy tone bother you?)

"Your words, inspired and God-breathed by the words in the Bible, empowered by God Himself, can change the world and the worldview of everyone in it."

HEAVENLY POV

The beautifully written words in Hebrews 12:1–2 tell us that we are surrounded by a cloud of witnesses, living on earth and in heaven. Christian writers on mission have set their goals: to please their heavenly audience. God is the audience before whom we bow and seek approval. We write because we are on mission for God and God alone. For years the Old Testament foretold stories about Jesus Christ. After they set the scene, New Testament writers told first-person accounts of Him! Imagine their sense of privilege to walk on earth with their Messiah!

Finally, we live as Christian writers in the era of the church. Step into position to write for Him in a new era so that Christ can be glorified *now*. When Jesus was on earth, He performed many signs and wonders. Yet He tells us in John 14:12 that Christians with faith will be able to do greater things. We live in a world of unlimited opportunities to spread the gospel. In the last few years unreached people groups are coming to know Jesus Christ in large numbers, more than ever in the history of the church.

You are a part of the worldwide opening of communications that offer instant evangelism to all the corners of the earth! And what you write echoes in the mansions of heaven, where homes are being prepared for all those who suddenly change their worldview and look through the eyes of Christ at a hurting world. Your children's stories can lead youth and children in your church to glorify God. Your adult fiction can offer a good cry in a story of redemption and spiritual growth.

As a result, your reader takes a giant leap of spiritual maturity and begins to glorify God through his own redemption and growth. His or her worldview expands, and men and women all over the world will be doing a 180-degree turn from seeing with the eyes of the world to seeing with the eyes of Christ. A Christ-centered worldview makes the difference. Men and women from all over the world don't still seek the applause of the secular public in materialistic nations, but seek the approval of their heavenly Father in heaven, who is our audience. Our total audience.

In John 1:45, Philip told Nathanael, "We have found the one Moses wrote about in the Law and about whom the prophets also wrote—Jesus of Nazareth." Philip and the early disciples had an explosive worldview. For years they had read the words of Moses, who was a writer—like you—and they had also read what the Old Testament prophets had written; and after the influence of those words, they were ready to receive the truth of Almighty God and the mystery of the gospel, namely Jesus, who came to earth to die for their sins! He died for *our sins* as twenty-first-century writers.

We write so our readers also will have an explosion of their

ONE WORLDVIEW CHANGED

One young woman asked her family and friends to give her "white umbrella" shower and wedding gifts to a restoration center for abused girls. Her fiancé agreed.

"It was great. No one brought a gift to the wedding because they'd already sent something for the girls. For us the focus was on our exchange of vows before God, not getting gifts for ourselves. It was a special way to show what we stand for." It was a memorable, beautiful night—the perfect start for the Love Gives Way campaign (thewhiteumbrellacampign .com/video/#Love).

worldviews! We pray for a pivotal turn toward Christ. We live for that day when a reader will read our words and all of a sudden they get it! They understand the mystery they've been reading about for years. Their view of the world shifts to a *Christview*, a worldview seen from the perspective of Christ! They see the poor through Jesus' eyes. They have compassion on a sinful young man or woman as Jesus would have had compassion. Just as the words of Moses and the prophets, just as the words of the New Testament apostles, *your* words, inspired and God-breathed by the words in the Bible, empowered by God Himself, will change the world and the worldview of everyone in it!

Author Bruce Wilkinson prayed a certain prayer for years. Then he wrote a little book, *The Prayer of Jabez*, which showed a Christ-centered worldview. Instead of building an empire on the book's profits and resting on his laurels, he and his extended family moved to Africa to serve a missions purpose. Now these were writers on mission!

For other books about focusing on a Christian worldview, go online and search for *The White Umbrella* by Mary Frances Bowley, *The Circle Maker* by Mark Batterson, and *Crazy Love* by Francis Chan.

THE MISSIONARY IN YOU

1. Have you ever seen anyone's worldview change? How did that experience influence your writing perspective?
2. For people with which kind of worldview is God nudging you to write?
3. What is your dream or mission statement for what God may do with your writing?
4. Would you recommend other books for writers? If so, share that information with your writer friends.

THE WRITER IN YOU

1. As you write, how will you determine your point of view?

2. Explain how you think your clear communication in writing can have an effect on heaven.

3. Why is second-person plural POV (*we, us, our, ours*) less offensive to non-Christians than second-person singular POV (*you, your, yours*)? Name several ways you think your writing can be attractive to a non-Christian audience rather than repulsive.

4. Which idea in this chapter is your favorite new idea?

A WRITER'S PRAYER

O Lord, give me the proper point of view in my writing. Help my Christian fiction or nonfiction to be an influence by giving a different worldview to those who don't know You. May I even influence the joy in heaven as new people come to know You. May my words share truth from my spirit, tell them about Your Spirit, and witness to their spirits. Open their hearts to change their worldview to a Christview. In Jesus' name, amen.

The Basics of Writing from a Christian Worldview

WRITING FROM CHRIST'S VIEW—HOW TO WRITE WITH CHRIST PERSPECTIVE

The one who received the seed that fell among the thorns is the man who hears the word, but the worries of this life and the deceitfulness of wealth choke it, making it unfruitful. But the one who received the seed that fell on good soil is the man who hears the word and understands it. He produces a crop, yielding a hundred, sixty or thirty times what was sown.

MATTHEW 13:22–23

Fourteen-year-old Gloria Simms was the captain of her middle school volleyball team. She poured her heart and soul into the team and they won several championships. Gloria was excited about the team, and played hard at every game. People congratulated her on each win. She participated in awards ceremonies where she accepted MVP and leadership honors, accepted accolades from many older teens and younger children who admired her. Immediately Gloria's mother noticed a self-focus and an inward pride that disturbed her. Since Mr. Simms worked late almost every night, Mrs. Simms came home from work tired and overwhelmed with dinner to prepare, two other siblings' homework to oversee, and other household chores to complete. She had little time to pay attention to Gloria, who seemed happy communicating on electronic devices and playing computer games.

When two of Gloria's closest church friends stopped coming over, her mother talked with them in the neighborhood one day.

"Her popularity has gone to her head, Mrs. Simms," one friend said.

Another joined the conversation: "She's stuck up . . . thinks she's better than all of us. Maybe she had too much success too soon. . . . Whatever it is, she's not even going out for the volleyball team—or anything else—at the high school."

Instead of playing sports or hanging out with Christian friends, Gloria had begun turning inward. She wanted new clothes, new shoes, new club memberships, and one new hairstyle after another. She was interested in tanning booths, elliptical equipment, and treadmills at expensive gyms with personal trainers. She skipped upward through a stack of more expensive electronic devices from flip phones to smartphones, and from BlackBerrys to Androids. She upgraded and added the newest apps as fast as her parents could provide the funds. They protested, but gave in reluctantly to her demands since new items made her happy and decreased family friction. The electronic communication made Gloria more withdrawn. She stopped talking at mealtimes and refused to play with her brothers and sisters. Mr. Simms blamed his wife, who also had pushed for more money, bigger houses, and country club memberships. She blamed her husband because he was never there to be a loving father to his family.

One day Gloria disappeared. When her parents investigated, some of her new friends told them she had gone to a large city nearby where an older boyfriend had promised her a job with a large salary.

The Simms family never found where Gloria went, though they took time off work, searched every street in the large city, and offered a reward. Their state had a strong law against human trafficking, but no one could prove where Gloria was or who took her away. The unhappy parents are still waiting, looking at every young woman they see, hoping one day Gloria will be able to return home.

Gloria was a sad example of someone whose worldview was too fragile to hold on to hope during a storm. Like the seed that fell among thorns, Gloria and her family experienced the deceitfulness of wealth, which choked the life out of their family. Her parents regretted not being closer to her in her middle school, since they focused on possessions and earning more money rather than a Christian perspective on life. A materialistic worldview was the enemy of this family, destroying each of its members eventually with alcohol, drugs, and other social issues.

CHRISTIAN WORLDVIEW AS A WRITER ON MISSION

As you read true stories like the one above, your heart might be broken for families like the Simms family. Recognizing trouble in the Simms household may encourage you to write as a ministry to troubled families. Regardless of the details, as you decide on topics for your writing efforts, your subject matter will grow out of your worldview. One focus of a Christian writer is to reconcile an opposite or errant worldview with a Christ-centered worldview. As God leads, your words can close the gap of miscommunication and help readers to accept Jesus as their Savior and form a healthy spiritual worldview. As you serve Christ through your writing, your missions and ministry focus may be an aim for a wider vision— even world evangelization.

Part of your search for topics or a focused aim may be to look at all the facets of your worldview. If your worldview includes a set of filters to exclude non-Christian habits and thoughts, exactly which kinds of filters narrow your worldview? Many theologians agree that you have three parts: body, soul, and spirit. Picture these in three concentric circles, with *body* on the outside; *soul* in the middle circle; and *spirit* in the inner, smaller circle.

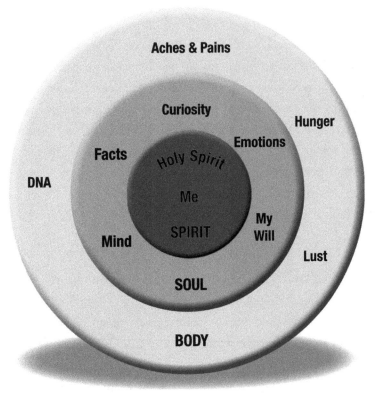

B BODY

The form and function of our bodies sometimes determine our focus. For instance, you may decide to write about a disease you or your family has. Physical urges such as hunger, thirst, or pain, etc., affect your focus. Other physical factors will influence your passion for certain topics related to the physical condition.

S SOUL

The next smaller circle, the soul, includes your will and emotions. Your intellectual mind, a curiosity about new ideas, your education, and all the memorized facts learned through it make up a part of your soul. Which topics found in our soul would be included as a focus for your writing?

s SPIRIT

Finally, in the inner circle, in your spirit, lies the Grand Central Station of your being. Watchman Nee says the spirit is the deep-core place where your spirit "mingles" with the Holy Spirit of the Living God. God has to peel away all the other layers of (1) physical yearnings and issues with the body; (2) emotional issues, mental battles, and empirical/intellectual facts of your soul; and (3) selfishness, rebellion, and spiritual warfare in your inner spirit where you are capable of communicating with God. Because He is Spirit, His power controls all the spiritual facets of your life and takes control of them, as you willingly give up control. When you worship or pray, your spirit *mingles* with your Lord's Holy Spirit, and as a writer, you are able to discern His choices for your writing and choose a moral, godly focus for them.

> **YOUR PERSONAL WORLDVIEW**
> "Everyone has a worldview, a way of making sense of the world and our lives in it."
>
> —THE LATE CHUCK COLSON, COLSON CENTER FOR CHRISTIAN WORLDVIEW
>
> Another Colson Web site includes the Worldview Gym, where readers can work out at spiritual exercises to learn and grow in their Christian worldview. (colsoncenter.org)

MINGLING WITH GOD

Before all Christian authors write, whether a simple letter to their adult children or a giant dissertation on maturity in the Christian life, they must draw aside from all the *physical* issues of pain, hunger, thirst, sexual, or other urges and all the inner-*soul* issues of social connections, mental problems, or feelings of guilt or inadequacy, and open up their *spirits* to mingle with God. At times God has to "crack us open," to use a Watchman Nee phrase, so that our spirits are tender and open to mingling. In *The Circle Maker*, Mark Batterson tells the legend of a spiritual leader who drew a circle around himself in the dust to pray until God provided answers to his prayer. God is still calling His people to spirit-mingling prayer. He says in Revelation 3:20, "Here I am! I stand at the door and knock! If anyone hears my voice and opens the door, I will come in and eat with him, and he with me."

 PHYSICAL

The world today cries out for a God circle. Writers have the power to draw such a circle and call others to join God in a circle of their own. People of all kinds today display a tremendous need that is critical: they need fellowship with His Spirit. They have covered themselves with such a physical shell that no one can crack them open.

Think about what your critical physical shell might be: the need for new shoes and jewelry, the latest computer apps, the newest innovation in electronic communication, a new car, or membership to any sort of club. Do you submit to control over you by a spouse, a child, or a friend that is influencing you toward the physical instead of the spiritual? What about your own personal purity? Can you admit today that your physical shell includes a raunchy television show or pornography from a certain Web site?

How about your job? Would you do anything to stay at the level where you are or to rise to the next level? Your worldview influences the way you think about your salary. Making a living as a writer is a good goal which provides physical needs for you and your family. But every *on-mission* Christian writer will willingly accept God's niche for him or her in the writing world and submit to God's will for career choices. Tithing, community generosity, and giving to just causes are part of the stewardship of God's gifts. He knows everything you and your family need and He is faithful to provide. His Word says, "The Lord will open the heavens, the storehouse of his bounty, to . . . bless all the work of your hands" (Deuteronomy 28:12).

May God have mercy on our souls when we cover ourselves with materialism and physical needs and turn our backsides to God Almighty.

E EMOTIONAL/MENTAL

Have you noticed that the world all around you is crying out for sanity? Think of all the things you have seen in the media, in schools, in businesses, and even in churches that make you say to your best friend or spouse, "This is insane! I never thought I'd see this in my lifetime" or "The world has gone crazy! How could this happen?" The question is, What has happened to our wills and emotions?

Our social and intellectual skills have experienced a mental lapse; we have emphasized self-esteem instead of hard work, sacrifice, and servanthood. We observe a society that is unwilling to give itself to a worthy cause. Or our worthy cause is a sham, fallen in disgrace. How many organizations or people have you seen fall from grace? Sometimes our inner curiosity becomes distorted and sick. It's not that we intend to sin, but some of us are just curious and slowly fall down the slippery slope toward disobedience to God's Spirit and worse behavior. Good morals fall by the wayside, pushed aside by meaningless trivia, selfishness that is admired, and comedy that honors bathroom humor. Snide remarks about illegal drugs and/or warped sexual innuendos are the stuff we find on the best-seller or top ten list. The entertainment industry honors art that emphasizes all the above instead of wholesome ideals that make the world a better place. Our middle circle, our emotional and mental stratum, covers our spirits with banal shallowness.

Although we are Christians, we
sometimes can hardly recognize
the Holy Spirit because He is
drowning in the center cores of
our hearts, which are often covered with the world's garbage!

"Our iron wills are made of wispy, wrinkled tissue paper."

We don't want to believe that the paragraph above pertains to us as Christian writers, yet at times, even *strong* Christian writers find ourselves jealous of other Christian writers, when God gives them success or an assignment we wish we had. Paul says His purpose is that church members (including you and me) "may be encouraged in heart and united in love" (Colossians 2:2). His heart must be broken when He sees our petty jealousy over writing assignments for Him.

Where is our iron will, which should reside in the middle layer of our beings? Sometimes it's made of wispy, wrinkled tissue paper. We are nowhere near where we should be in our dedication and spiritual development because our lives are cluttered with physical and emotional hard shells.

May God have mercy on our souls when we cover ourselves with crumbly paper-moon thinking and entertaining ourselves with trivia, while an almighty God is asking us to ignore such ignorance and come to Him for integrity and solid morality.

SPIRIT

Only in the shrinking heart-core inner circle of your spirit can God's Holy Spirit mingle with yours. There dwells the real you. As a writer, you can invite Him inside now. He wants to heal your inner core as He heals you and me from the inside out, through the spirit-enlarging Holy Spirit.

Take a hard look at your inner spirit now. Ask God to crack it open and see what is lurking there. We hardly recognize ourselves,

do we? Most of us have fooled so many other people that we've
even fooled ourselves into thinking our lies were truth. Or are you
right now denying you've ever told any lies?

Have you ever pretended to be a fabulous Christian and even
refused to accept the truth that you are a shivering beggar in the
cold because you can't bring yourself to go inside and warm yourself
by the fire of the Holy Spirit? Every one of us is a shivering beggar.
Many of us are so prideful or afraid of God that we can't step up to
His face and tell Him the absolute truth, which He can see lurking
down deep in our spirits anyway. Perhaps God is calling you to be
the only remnant of integrity and humility in the fallen world all
around you. May we stand firmly
in our Christian worldview,
never allowing the materialistic,
physical world to warp us. May
we never find it difficult to let
God take control so that we can
become *writers on mission* for Him.

> "It's hard to obey because
> obedience requires ripping off
> the first two layers that have
> superglued themselves to our
> spirits and won't let go!"

The language of the inner
spirit is thanksgiving and obedience—two things we often hate
to face. We want the thanks, the accolades, and the admiration.
Sometimes it's hard to be humble enough to worship Him in spirit
and truth. Paul says,

> *I pray that out of his glorious riches he may strengthen you with
> power through His Spirit in your inner being, so that Christ may
> dwell in your hearts through faith . . . that you may be filled to
> the measure of all the fullness of God* (EPHESIANS 3:16–17, 19).

God's Spirit in your inner being will dwell there through faith, as
you are filled with the fullness of His words to pour out in your
writing.

After we write a passage of beautiful words, we read it over and over. It becomes our idol, and sometimes we worship it. Though we would never admit it, we envy God occasionally and hope to steal just a bit of His greatness and transfer it to us. We despise the discipline He insists on requiring. It's hard to obey because obedience requires ripping off the first two layers that have superglued themselves to our spirits and won't let go!

OBSESSED

Even we who are strong Christians, godly writers, who have taken a stand for Christ, can fall prey to this watered-down spirit life. If we're expecting to write with the worldview, or filter, of God's eyes, then it is imperative that we give attention to worldview maintenance.

Besides refining our Christ-centered worldview through prayer, how do we maintain our worldview? It requires two things:

1. We use our iron wills to say no to Satan. Do you remember the day Jesus looked Satan in the eye and said, "Away from me, Satan! For it is written: 'Worship the Lord your God, and serve him only'" (Matthew 4: 10)? We can do as Jesus did. Totally deny any evil creeping into our writing. You and I as Christian writers can set our iron wills and take a stand *against* evil and *for* righteousness.

2. We walk in the Spirit and not in the world, as Paul says in Galatians 5:25. We turn our backs on worldliness. We follow His two words of advice in Colossians 3:1–2, 5: First, "Set your hearts . . . [and] minds on things above"; and second, "Put to death . . . whatever belongs to your earthly nature." We decide not to cave in to the worldliness and superficiality of some current popular writings. We can say no to a watered-down gospel and stay focused on our mission: to tell every person in the world about Jesus Christ who died for each of them.

Our neighbors will think we're crazy, but we can deny ourselves the decadence the world provides. Years ago a book called *Magnificent*

Obsession centered around a man who promised God he would serve Him the rest of his life, living in unselfish service to others. He lost friends because of his obsession with serving Christ. Most people didn't understand him. In *Crazy Love*, Francis Chan says Christian people are *obsessed-with-Jesus* people who know pride is always a battle. Obsessed people make *themselves less known* and *Christ more known*. They orient themselves around eternity and are not fixed on what is in front of them. As a writer, will you *show, not tell,* us that you are settled, committed, and passionate about your obsessive love for Christ?

SPIRIT VIEWING

The everyday Christian vision of a writer on mission flows through his or her fiction and nonfiction. To get down to basics, your fiction requires a well-described setting; interesting, three-dimensional characters; and a compelling plot (with subplots sprinkled in, as needed). But far more important is the Spirit of God shining through your words. Focus on your mission.

Your nonfiction requires a persuasive style that is absolutely sold out to Jesus. Paul says, "Make the most of every opportunity. Let your conversation be always full of grace, seasoned with salt, so that you may know how to answer everyone" (Colossians 4:5–6). Share your salt.

Everything you write grows out of your worldview: your diction demands a certain level of civility, the ethics of your main fictional characters are on a higher plane, the integrity of your suggestions in a how-to-book will not compromise the morality of the reader who is following your directions.

Your *platform* as a writer will focus on God. As you create a name or identity, you will show your passion for God. Rick Warren is known as the *Purpose-Driven Life* advocate. Henry Blackaby is known for *Experiencing God*. Allison Bottke is the *God Allows U-Turns* writer. Edna Ellison is known as the Christian mentoring guru.

Linda Gilden is known for her *Love Notes in Lunchboxes* as she shares God's love. Your business cards or bookmarks are places to focus on a Christian message for the casual reader who may pick one up at a book signing. As you accumulate data from your Facebook fans, tweet on Twitter, or gather recommendations from colleagues on LinkedIn, as a part of your platform, focus on *His plans* for each of those social networks. Display a strong Christian worldview in your monthly newsletter or blog. When you book yourself as a speaker, make sure you have something significant to say that highlights your missions focus. Your fiction and nonfiction, your platform and marketing will focus on an obsessed-with-Jesus worldview.

THE MISSIONARY IN YOU

1. How do you see yourself as a carrier of the good news, proclaiming peace and salvation, praising God through the words you select to write? Describe.

2. Recall a time when you felt God's Spirit mingling with your spirit. What happened?

3. How do you believe a Christian writer demonstrates an obsessed-with-Jesus worldview?

THE WRITER IN YOU

1. Describe a character you might write about who has a hardened shell over his body (physical self) and soul (will, mind, and emotional self).

2. On the adjacent page, match (by writing the letter in the left column blank) the words in the left column with the words on the right. Then explain why you chose the words you selected. How do the words identify the worldview/age/era of the speakers?

3. Write a promise to God about your own worldview maintenance:

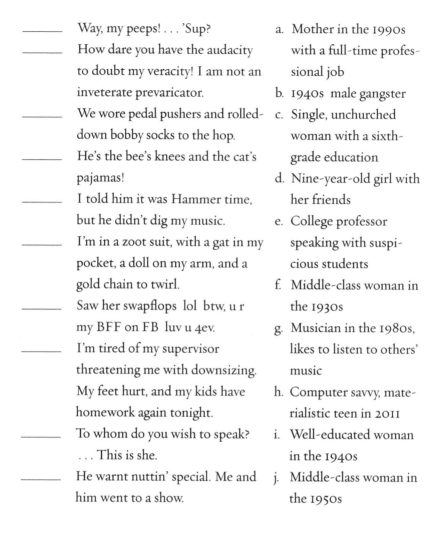

——— Way, my peeps! . . . 'Sup?

——— How dare you have the audacity to doubt my veracity! I am not an inveterate prevaricator.

——— We wore pedal pushers and rolled-down bobby socks to the hop.

——— He's the bee's knees and the cat's pajamas!

——— I told him it was Hammer time, but he didn't dig my music.

——— I'm in a zoot suit, with a gat in my pocket, a doll on my arm, and a gold chain to twirl.

——— Saw her swapflops lol btw, u r my BFF on FB luv u 4ev.

——— I'm tired of my supervisor threatening me with downsizing. My feet hurt, and my kids have homework again tonight.

——— To whom do you wish to speak? . . . This is she.

——— He warnt nuttin' special. Me and him went to a show.

a. Mother in the 1990s with a full-time professional job

b. 1940s male gangster

c. Single, unchurched woman with a sixth-grade education

d. Nine-year-old girl with her friends

e. College professor speaking with suspicious students

f. Middle-class woman in the 1930s

g. Musician in the 1980s, likes to listen to others' music

h. Computer savvy, materialistic teen in 2011

i. Well-educated woman in the 1940s

j. Middle-class woman in the 1950s

Answers: 1. d, 2. e, 3. j, 4. f, 5. g, 6. b, 7. h, 8. a, 9. i, 10. c
10 correct: know the worldview/age/era
7–9 correct: know some of the characteristics
4–6 correct: don't know these characteristics
1–3 correct: need to research people of all age levels

A WRITER'S PRAYER

Lord, show me how to share my worldview with others. Help me to identify those who have another worldview without You. Show me the ones You want me to influence. Lord, I accept the challenge to be obsessed with Jesus, who gives me courage to share my worldview with them through my written words. Help me introduce them to Your Spirit within me. I acknowledge that it is Your Spirit that touches them and I am a helpless writer without You. In Jesus' name, amen.

C H A P T E R &7

The Basics of Relationships in Writing

REACHING OTHERS — THE INFLUENTIAL STAGE
OF WRITING FOR CHRIST

With all humility and gentleness, with patience, showing forbearance to one another in love, being diligent to preserve the unity of the Spirit in the bond of peace.

EPHESIANS 4:2–3

We have a relationship guidebook that not only gives us a history of relationships but also provides instruction as to how to develop relationships.

In Genesis, the first relationships on earth are recorded. God and Adam had a close and pure relationship when God created the first man for the purpose of fellowship. After that came animals and we can be pretty sure Adam had a close relationship with his animals. After all, they were the only beings on earth for a time. Then God created Eve and the relationship of man to woman, husband to wife, was created.

The entire Bible is a book of relationships beginning with the relationship of God to man. That should be a clue as to which relationship is the most important one of all—your relationship with God. The Bible is a story of God's relationship with us, His children. He loved us so much He sent His Son Jesus to die for us. But even before Jesus was born, God had a relationship with His people, beginning with Adam.

THE IMPORTANCE OF RELATIONSHIPS IN WRITING

Every day we deal with other people, people with whom we have relationships. Husbands, wives, children, parents, friends, co-workers, and acquaintances. And every time we are in the company of someone else, we have the opportunity to encourage him or her and leave a mark on his or her life.

When you are called to be a writer, another category of very important people enters your life—readers. You must know, understand, and care about your readers very deeply. As a beginning writer, one of the most important things you can do is to build a following. Write in such a way that people want to read everything you write. Get to know your audience and they will get to know you. Let them know you are trustworthy and they will remain with you.

6 GOD

Your relationship with God is the foundational relationship for all others. When we accept Jesus into our lives and know Him as our Savior, that relationship is guaranteed through eternity. All other earthly relationships are very precious to us, but they are expendable. In the scope of eternity, we must cling to the one relationship that matters most—that of our relationship with Jesus.

Just as you spend time with an earthly friend to get to know him or her better, spending time with God enhances and deepens your relationship with Him. When we know Him, we know we can trust Him and we work to exhibit His characteristics in our lives. Being aware of His daily presence with us wherever we go gives us confidence and assurance of our calling as writers. Knowing He is sitting at the desk with us as we write gives us inspiration and focus.

Talking to God is another way of connecting our spirits with His. First Thessalonians 5:17 tells us to "pray continually." That means we can have a running conversation about everything that is going on in our lives. God

"Only when we are finding our ultimate satisfaction in God are we able to relate rightly to one another."

—RICHARD D. AND
SHARON L PHILLIPS,
Holding Hands, Holding Hearts

is there and will listen and direct us. His presence is with us in writing as well as praying. In fact, as Christian writers it is even more important that we communicate with God. We are His messengers and our calling is to communicate His message to a lost world. We need His input in everything we write.

SELF

It may sound rather strange to talk about a relationship with yourself, but each person has a very definite opinion of himself or herself. If that opinion reflects a high self-esteem, everything is great and that person relates well to others. If a self-opinion is negative, that negative attitude will affect that person's relationships.

Someone with a negative opinion of himself or herself will lack self-confidence and approach relationships in a tentative, timid, and apprehensive manor. On the other hand, someone who is positive and confident will develop strong, lasting relationships with others.

Knowing who you are in Christ takes all the pressure off trying to be someone He did not create you to be. The relationship boosts your self-confidence, your self-image is more positive, and you interact with others in a more self-assertive way.

"For a long time I struggled," says SueLyn. "I never felt I was good enough. I never felt I could accomplish anything worthwhile." She smiles. "But then I realized all those feelings were insecurity that was a result of trying or wanting to be something other than what God made me to be. Once I spent some time with God and He showed me just how much He loved me just the way I was, I relaxed and began to enjoy who I really was."

SueLyn continues, "Once I got to that point, it didn't matter what kind of situation I found myself in, I could be comfortable. Often our boss takes the office staff out to lunch. All my co-workers are very chatty and outgoing. I am just the opposite. But I really enjoy going out with them and just listening to the conversation and not feeling obligated to enter in."

FAMILY

Family has several definitions in the dictionary. Probably the first thing most of us think about when we hear the word *family*, is mother, father, sisters, and brothers—blood relatives. But in the broader sense of the word, *family* can mean others with whom we have close and binding relationships.

The immediate family is, of course, just what we expect—those people whom God has put together. After choosing our mates, God gives us children to share our lives with and to nurture and guide as they grow. The immediate family is the group that you build lasting memories with from the day you are born until you move away from home. Even if you are away from home for years, memories will reconnect you quickly when you are reunited.

Your extended family is usually thought of as just that—family that extends beyond the immediate family. This would include grandparents, aunts, uncles, and cousins. These are people you see as often as you can and who love you just because you are family. Many people have extended family all over the country.

As Christians, another very important family to us is the family of God. Many Christians are part of a church family and worship with them regularly. But all of us as Christians are a part of an even larger family, *the family of God*. And whenever we encounter another believer, we are able to have instant fellowship because of the Holy Spirit that indwells us all.

Sometimes the hardest relationships to grow and maintain are the relationships with those we love and are with most of the time—our families. But despite the fact that those relationships can take work, they also provide us with many happy moments and memories.

Our family relationships can also provide many wonderful examples for our stories and inspire us to write. Parents realize how much God is teaching them about life through the eyes of their children. In-law relationships take work and adjustment as children of different upbringing are added to the family. Whatever your family circumstances, writing material abounds. However, remember to guard those relationships carefully and don't write about anything pertaining to your family without permission and the wisest discretion.

OTHERS

Every relationship is different because people are different and interact in different ways.

We have close friends whom we have known for years and have very deep relationships. Why? Because we have spent many years getting to know each other and understanding each other. We have been together, eaten meals together, and know what things we enjoy doing together.

One year Sandra's family hosted a foreign student in their home. This ten-year-old student was part of a Christian choir that traveled around the United States ministering and raising funds for their organization. Gwen's family also hosted a student.

Because Sandra worked at a public school and Gwen worked at the church where the children went to school when they were in town, Gwen picked up Sandra's little girl every day to take her to school. They lived close together and it was easy for Gwen to make that stop.

One day Gwen started out as usual. Her foreign student, Kim, and her five-year-old son were with her. They chatted as they continued to the church. As they turned into the church's driveway, Gwen's student from India said, "Mom, what about Annie (Sandra's student)? We forgot her!"

Gwen gasped and gave quick instructions to her two children as she let them out at the church. Turning around, she quickly returned to Sandra's house to pick up Annie (who didn't even realize Gwen hadn't come yet because she was watching American cartoons!).

Once safely back to church/school, Gwen spent the rest of the day trying to figure out how she was going to tell Sandra of her mistake. Gwen loved Annie and she had not forgotten her on purpose. But she knew her good friend loved this child like one of her own and the thought of Gwen's forgetting to pick Annie up could be hard to take.

But Sandra was very understanding. "No harm done! Annie was fine. It's not like she was standing on the street corner in three feet of snow. Just please don't forget her tomorrow!"

Gwen appreciated Sandra's forgiveness and was sure she would remember Annie from then on.

The next day when Gwen, her student, and her son gathered their things and went out the door to Gwen's big, red van, they were excited about another day at school.

"Mom, what is that?" Kim asked.

Gwen looked up. Attached to the antenna of her van was a yellow balloon with one word written across it: ANNIE! The threesome began to giggle. And they giggled all the way to Annie's house with the yellow balloon bobbing up and down inside the big, red van.

Sandra and Gwen have built a friendship over many years. Sandra's lighthearted way of showing her forgiveness is an indication of the depth of their relationship.

But what about people you don't have long-term relationships with? How do you build a friendship that will stay strong?

Marilyn had developed a relationship with the woman at the drive-through window at her favorite restaurant. Each time she went, Rachel took her order and met her at the window with a smile.

"How are you today?" she asked.

As the two women's friendship grew, they learned more about each other and their families. Rachel began to share that hard times had fallen on her family. Over the course of the conversations, Marilyn discovered that Rachel didn't know the Lord and she was trying to manage life all alone.

"Would you like to know my best friend?" Marilyn asked. "He is always there, gives me peace during the hard times, and the best part of all is that I will live forever with Him."

Rachel had a puzzled look on her face.

"It's Jesus!" Marilyn exclaimed and shared with Rachel how she could know Jesus as her Lord and Savior. So a relationship that began with a drive-through order ended up introducing Rachel to eternal life.

God has a purpose for all our relationships, even those that seem to be casual acquaintances.

Two people are better off than one, for they can help each other succeed. If one person falls, the other can reach out and help. But someone who falls alone is in real trouble. Likewise, two people lying close together can keep each other warm.

But how can one be warm alone? A person standing alone can be attacked and defeated, but two can stand back-to-back and conquer. Three are even better, for a triple-braided cord is not easily broken.

ECCLESIASTES 4:9–12 (NLT)

READERS

When God called you to be a writer and began equipping you for the task, you probably started reading all the writing books you could find, attending writers conferences, and picking the brains of other writers. You sought writers in your area and asked how to go about the business of writing and where to find gigs. You wanted to know it all!

But did you think about your readers?

One of the important questions on any book proposal that also applies to articles is, who is your target audience?

New writers often think the correct answer to that question is, all the Christians in the world. But the reality is that when you give that answer, you are indicating you don't know who your audience is at all; you are just hoping everybody will buy your book. And you think if you indicate all readers as your target audience, you will fool your editor into thinking you are writing the first book in the world to fit everyone. But that is not true. Editors want to know whom you see as your primary reader. What person do you see buying your book at the bookstore and then calling all like-minded friends to tell them they must have your book?

The target audience is usually a very small niche audience. Instead of writing to all the moms in the world, you might list your target audience as all the moms in the world with children under age five. Sometimes you may be even more specific. If you are writing about a unique situation, find groups that would be interested in that subject. For instance, if you have a child with dyslexia and you struggled in the beginning as you learned how to help him or her learn, put those struggles into an article or book. Then you can tell the editor about your personal experience as well as your affiliation with national organizations that are dedicated to helping those with dyslexia and their families.

In the beginning, most writers write an article or book proposal and try to find a market once it is complete. But you don't see many experienced writers doing that, because they have learned if you know your audience and write specifically to that audience, you will have a much greater opportunity of reaching the hearts of the people and making sales.

Many writing teachers suggest writing as if you are writing to one specific individual. So, if you are writing nonfiction on the best way to organize your kitchen, think of a good friend who is constantly saying she needs to get organized. Picture her as you write and write as if giving her the instruction she needs to overcome her clutter. If you are writing fiction, weave your story with your target reader in mind. Some people even go so far as to visualize their readers and/or cut their pictures out of magazines to post near the computer.

In order to know what material will mean the most to your audience and will meet their felt needs, you should know who your audience is. If you have an idea of who your audience is, you will be able to write in ways that will best influence them and help them understand the concepts in your material.

When you are looking for advice or instruction, don't you seek out someone you already have a relationship with?

When you start building relationships with your readers, you must prove yourself trustworthy. Readers want to know they can trust the author they are reading, especially when the author is writing about life-changing subjects.

Building a bonding relationship is the reason you should pay close attention to details, even in the small things. If your readers learn they can trust you through the small things, they will know they can trust you in the bigger ones. So make integrity a habit and part of your character.

As Christian writers, you have an even greater responsibility to your readers than secular authors because everything you write must be written from a Christian worldview and contain truth wherever you have the opportunity to share it. This doesn't mean the word *Jesus* has to be on every page. But it does mean that you are keenly aware that some of your readers may not know Him and that the words you write will honor Him in every way.

A well-known Christian ghostwriter once recounted her experience writing a biography of a man who took Bibles into areas where they were not allowed by law. She wanted to be 100 percent accurate with her writing. She went to the man's hometown and studied places where he lived and worked. She walked the streets around his former house so she could get the feel of the setting. She wrote about it with impeccable accuracy.

When the book came out, she began receiving mail from her readers. One was particularly special. A reader wrote, "My hometown is the town you wrote about in your book. I was amazed at how right on target you were with your description. I went to the same school. I shopped in the same stores. I walked the same streets. You didn't miss anything. I knew if you were so accurate about the things I was familiar with, I could trust what you said about Jesus Christ. I have accepted Him into my life. Thank you!"

Integrity is an important part of being a Christian and it should overflow into everything you write.

THE MISSIONARY IN YOU

1. Do you have a burning message in your heart that you want to share with others?

2. Do you enjoy meeting new people and feel genuinely concerned for their welfare?

3. Do you spend time growing your relationship with God so that you can be a good missional writer?

4. Do you work hard to build good relationships with those you meet?

THE WRITER IN YOU

1. Does your writing spring from the overflow of a close relationship with God?

2. Do you find that your relationships are a springboard for good stories? Do you take those relationships seriously and work hard to create trust so you can impart truth to your readers?

3. When you write about your family, are you careful to have their permission and refrain from writing anything derogatory?

4. Do you study the craft of writing so that everything you write is the best it can possibly be? We know we have a great message and we should present that message in the best possible form.

A WRITER'S PRAYER

Dear God, I want to know You so well that our relationship is the foundation for everything else I do. I especially want that to be true of my writing. Fill me in such a way that I can overflow and bless my readers in a fresh new way. And may they see You in every word. In the name of Your precious Son. Amen.

C H A P T E R 8

Developing Strong Personal Connections

UNDERSTANDING OTHERS—HOW TO WRITE
THROUGH PERSONAL RELATIONSHIPS

In as much as it depends on you, if at all possible, live at peace with all men.

ROMANS 12:18

Paul knew we had a part in building strong relationships. That's why he encouraged us to do whatever it took to live at peace with those around us. But how can you do that?

WRITING THROUGH PERSONAL RELATIONSHIPS

From the time you are born, you are told you are unique. You are not like anyone else. God made you to be who you are and no one else is exactly like you.

Part of our uniqueness is in our personalities. Unless we understand characteristics of each different personality, we may have trouble getting along and building relationships with those whose personalities are not like ours. Most people have a dominant personality but can exhibit traits of all the others.

Strong personal connections with those around us begin with understanding that God made each of us differently and being exactly who we are. Connecting with our readers works the same way. Unless we understand how each personality reads and perceives and interprets our material, we will lose some of our readers along the way.

Researchers have done many studies on the personalities. Many of them were similar; they just chose different words to refer to them. Hippocrates recognized that people had very different personality traits and a pattern seemed to be related to body parts. He labeled the four personalities as melancholy, choleric, sanguine, and phlegmatic. Others have used animal names, adjectives, or just letters to describe personalities.

MELANCHOLY—THE SERIOUS, PURPOSEFUL PERSONALITY

The melancholy, purposeful personality is often misunderstood. Always appearing serious and regularly accused of needing to "lighten up," this introverted personality really enjoys life, family, and friends.

One of the most asked questions at Fran's house is, "Mom, are you mad or is something wrong?"

"I am not mad," says Fran. "I love my family. In fact, there is nowhere I'd rather be than serving and playing with my family. But I have to admit I don't always smile and act like I am enjoying it. I guess I need to practice letting my face show how I feel on the inside!"

Not one to volunteer for up-front positions, the melancholy is a great behind-the-scenes person who pays great attention to detail. When working with someone with this personality, you can give him or her a list of instructions and know they will follow them explicitly. Often perfectionists, melancholy people have to work hard not to impose their perfectionist tendencies on those around them or to judge others by their personal, perfectionist standards.

Writing is a great career for the melancholy person. Because of his or her love of research and deep thinking, the melancholy writer is perfectly content sitting alone in a room diligently working on a project.

Do you think this is your personality? If you answer yes to some of the questions below, you could be a melancholy personality.

Are you a good listener?

Are you happier at home with a good book than in a roomful of energetic friends?

When given a task, do you immediately create a plan and begin following it?

Is it hard for you to forget and forgive those who hurt you or someone in your family?

When you attend Bible study, do you leave wishing the facilitator had given you just a few more details about the Scripture?

Moses was a melancholy personality. When God called him to lead his people, his first reaction was, "Who, me? I can't possibly do that!"

CHOLERIC—THE POWERFUL,
IT'S-ALL-ABOUT-BUSINESS PERSONALITY

It is usually easy to spot a choleric personality. A choleric person likes to be in charge. He or she is quick to step up to the plate in a crisis or in a routine situation that seems to have no one to direct the activity.

Recently at a Vacation Bible School, a young man came down the hill too fast on his bicycle and ran into the church's metal air-conditioner cover. Shannon, a very powerful personality, ran immediately over to the young man and began administering first aid at the same time directing others in what to do.

"Call 911. We need an ambulance," she told one woman.

"I need some wet towels," she told another.

"Take the other children into the fellowship hall and sing songs with them."

This matter-of-fact personality doesn't like a lot of frivolity. Although he or she loves people and enjoys social activities, the "fluff" is not his or her favorite part. "Get to the point!" he or she might say if a conversation gets too lengthy and rambles. Or you may find a choleric person will not be very patient and begin finishing sentences for you!

Could you be a choleric personality? If any of these phrases describes you, there is probably a good chance you are.

You love to make lists and check off the things on it.

You don't need a lot of sleep and feel you always need to be doing something.

You are a good leader and are often asked to be in charge.

You are well organized.

You have been known to finish sentences for others when their stories and comments become too long and drawn out.

You love God with all your heart and work tirelessly for His kingdom.

Paul was a choleric, powerful personality. He took the lessons God gave him and put them in succinct, understandable form to share with others.

SANGUINE—THE PLAYFUL, FLY-BY-THE-SEAT-OF-MY-PANTS PERSONALITY

The fun-loving sanguine personality is easily recognizable. He or she is always the life of any party, demanding attention by loud, colorful clothes; constant storytelling; and has no lack of friends. He or she has never met a stranger and often comes home from a meeting with a new best friend. Everybody loves being with sanguine friends because they are spontaneous and never lack for something to do. Life is a party and if there is not enough celebration, a sanguine friend can create one!

Fred says, "Margie often rolls her eyes when I tell her the office group is going out to a movie together. She prefers a quiet evening at home with just a couple or two. But I love getting together with the office, our Sunday School class, or just the neighbors. It is so much fun to learn what is going on. People are so interesting!"

Fred and Margie were recently in a hotel elevator. Once they got in the elevator car, three more people shared the ride. Fred immediately instigated a conversation with one of them. Margie just stood silently, not even acknowledging the other folks with eye contact. When they exited the elevator, Fred had made a new friend and Margie was relieved the ride was over! Different perspectives of a one-minute experience because their personalities were different.

Could you be a sanguine, people person like Fred? Answer yes to some of the questions below and it's probably so.

Do you love a party—the more the merrier?

Are your clothes colorful and do they call attention to you?

Do you lack discretion about who you share your life with? After all, isn't it more important to have a good story than to worry about privacy?

When someone needs help, are you quick to volunteer?

Is your quiet time with God a struggle because sitting alone seems to not be lively enough for you?

Our biblical friend Peter is surely a sanguine, extrovert personality.

PHLEGMATIC—THE PEACEMAKER AND
EASYGOING PERSONALITY

Sometimes the phlegmatic, peaceful personality is viewed as lazy and withdrawn. But just because a person is quiet and doesn't interact very much doesn't mean he or she is uninterested in what is going on in the world.

The phlegmatic person is very relaxed but thinks deeply and loves to ponder things. He or she loves to come up with solutions to problems. Often the observer, he or she is content to watch people or watch the action. The phlegmatic, peaceful personality is just that—peaceful—and can get along with just about anybody.

"I don't know why he acts that way," melancholy Kelly said of her brother-in-law. "He ought to be thankful for our family and try to get along with everyone."

"He's really not so bad," said Kelly's phlegmatic brother, Ron. I really enjoy talking to him. You just have to understand he has his own way of doing things."

Kelly frowned. Her brother always saw the good side of people. Didn't he realize things should be done a certain way to be acceptable?

This personality loves to follow the directions of others they trust.

Are you a peaceful, phlegmatic personality? If these phrases describe you, you probably fit in the peaceful category.

You rarely show emotions.

You have lots of friends.

Some people think you are not enthusiastic enough.

You have more patience than most people.

When there is a disagreement in the family, you are the mediator.

Your relationship with God is steady, gentle, and gratifying.

Abraham exhibited traits of a phlegmatic personality.

This may be way more than you ever wanted to know about personalities. But if we are to communicate effectively with our readers, we need to understand that the way they digest information is different. We need to make sure our writing includes something for each personality.

The concept of the four basic personalities offers
us a tool by which we can take an honest look at our
strengths and our weaknesses and begin to rid our
lives of the behavior patterns which may be offensive
to those around us. When we as Christians become
aware of our weaknesses and prayerfully take them to
the Lord, we can allow the Holy Spirit to work in our
lives to make us more balanced and Christ-like.

—FLORENCE LITTAUER

FOR THE PURPOSEFUL, MELANCHOLY READER—Many readers are
melancholy. Why? Because they have a thirst for knowledge. They
love for you to share everything you know. People of this personality appreciate your research and often wish you had gone even more
deeply into your subject. If you write nonfiction, you may find that
melancholy readers will finish your book and then read others on
the subject to broaden their perspective. If you write fiction, these
readers are the ones who will cry with you and feel deeply through
your characters who become very real to them. They will also check
the details of your story to make sure they flow together properly.

FOR THE POWERFUL, CHOLERIC READER—These matter-of-fact
readers are thirsty for knowledge. They want information, pure
unadorned information. They don't care about all the flowery
words; they just want the facts. So for your choleric readers, don't
beat around the bush. For nonfiction writers, this group of readers
are the ones the bullets and lists are perfect for. In fiction, this
group includes your readers of historical fiction. They love to be
learning something while being entertained.

FOR THE PLAYFUL, SANGUINE READER—This group of readers
loves a good story. But you must engage them quickly or something
may come along that they think may be more fun than sitting still

with a book in their laps! Sanguine readers are creative and enjoy reading that incorporates creativity, whether nonfiction or fiction. Just remember to keep this group moving and surprised as you write!

THE PEACEFUL, PHLEGMATIC READER—For those in this group who like to read, they could be your biggest and most loyal fans. Phlegmatic readers will stay true to their favorite authors. They particularly love to lose themselves in a good novel that takes them to a place of relaxation and repose. They choose their nonfiction carefully according to their greatest interests.

Knowing a bit about the personalities enables you to create deeper fictional characters.

Once you determine the personality of your characters, you have guidelines for their actions, reactions, and speech. This can be freeing and speed things along as you write.

In nonfiction, keeping the personalities in mind as you write assures you have something for everyone. Your readers will appreciate your understanding that all readers are different and need different approaches to transmitting information. Use a combination of writing techniques to reach readers of all personalities.

What about you as the writer? Will understanding the personalities help you understand your own personality and why you write the way you do? Of course.

FOR THE PURPOSEFUL, MELANCHOLY WRITER—Pay close attention to your target audience.

Remember your readers who, unlike yourself, do not really want to know every little detail about everything. Do your research, use what you need, and save the rest for an in-depth article or for another book.

FOR THE POWERFUL, CHOLERIC WRITER—This group of writers is great at delivering information in a concise and clearly understood way. If you are in this group, you may need to add a little bit of warmth to your writing for the other personalities to stick with you. Choleric, powerful writers make excellent technical writers because they want to give you just the facts, often in a list form.

FOR THE PLAYFUL, SANGUINE WRITER—Writing is probably not your favorite thing to do. You can think of a dozen different things you should be doing besides writing. If that is you, develop a system of rewards that will give you incentive to stay in your chair and write. Once you have written a certain number of words or pages, reward yourself with a phone call to a friend or a short coffee break.

FOR THE PEACEFUL, PHLEGMATIC WRITER—Many peaceful, phlegmatic writers find it difficult to get started on projects. But once started they can stay focused and get lost in their subjects. Writing produced by this group is often genuine and gentle, warm and wonderful.

Perhaps such a great amount of information about personalities seems overkill in a chapter about personal connections. But the depth of understanding is directly related to the depth of the relationship.

Networking is an important part of being a writer. You will have relationships with other writers, editors, publishers, and more. Knowing their personalities and how you can relate to them will enable you to develop relationships with fewer misunderstandings and more lasting business relationships.

⁂

God embodies characteristics of all the personalities. The Scriptures give numerous examples of Jesus when He exhibits *traits of each personality*. Because God is all the personalities in One, He is wide open to receive us and to understand our thoughts and feelings based on who we are. We can have a deep relationship with God, the deepest of all.

JESUS, THE MELANCHOLY PERSONALITY—He was sensitive and wept when His friend died (John 11:35). He loved children and wanted to nurture them. He was organized and fed thousands on a hillside. Though busy about His ministry, He needed to get away by Himself occasionally.

JESUS, THE CHOLERIC PERSONALITY—He was a leader and people left their homes and families to follow Him. He accomplished much—He had a plan and followed it. He didn't shrink from confrontation; He stood up to the Roman leaders.

JESUS, THE SANGUINE PERSONALITY—Jesus loved being with people and even performed His first miracle at a party. He was a fabulous storyteller, often using parables to communicate truth. He was spontaneous. When He saw a need, He changed directions and met that need.

JESUS, THE PHLEGMATIC PERSONALITY—Jesus came to bring peace to the world. He was a mediator, the bridge between God and man. He cared enough to listen carefully to those He spoke to.

As writers, as friends, as family members, we must do our part to relate and interact with those around us. As Paul said in Romans 12:18, "As much as it depends on you."

The ball is in our courts. Will we get along with others? Will we write in a clear and understandable way? Can we deepen our relationships with God knowing He created us and understands us completely? To learn more about personalities, read *Personality Perspectives: Clues to Building Better Relationships* by Linda Gilden and Tama Westman or attend CLASSeminars' Personality Training (classeminars.org).

THE MISSIONARY IN YOU

1. Do you think much about your personality and how it affects everything you do? The way you present Jesus to others through your personal testimony will reflect your personality. Likewise, the way your message is received will be directly affected by the listener's personality.

2. Can you recall times when you reacted in a certain way because of your personality?

3. Now that you have a little better understanding of the personalities, can you develop closer relationships with others?

4. Connecting with others is important. Can you think of other factors that are important to building and growing relationships?

THE WRITER IN YOU

1. How important is it to know your reader and target audience?

2. When you are writing, if you think of people you know with each personality, does that help you visualize your readers?

3. What are the four basic personality types and how do they affect you as a writer?

4. Do you know what your dominant personality type is?

A WRITER'S PRAYER

Dear God, thank You for making me uniquely me. Help me to live within my strengths and work on my weaknesses. I know You are the One who created me and I thank You that I don't have to try to be anyone else. Give me a deeper understanding of my family and friends that leads to a deeper love for them. I want to exhibit Your love to everyone I meet. Amen.

The Basics of Communicating to Reach Others

WRITING TO SPREAD THE WORD— THE INTERACTION STAGE OF WRITING FOR CHRIST

You show that you are a letter from Christ, the result of our ministry, written not with ink but with the Spirit of the living God, not on tablets of stone but on tablets of human hearts.

2 CORINTHIANS 3:3

When Rose was in college, she finally got to the point in her schedule where she could take creative writing. She really wanted to be a writer despite her double major in French and religious education! Her creative writing teacher finally finished teaching all the basics and the time came for the class to try their hands at the writing thing.

Rose worked hard to perfect her essay and turned it in, knowing Mrs. Gambert's first comments would be glowing. It was a *Reader's Digest* shoo-in! Or so she thought.

But when the essay was returned to Rose, the only words on the paper were, "You have nice handwriting!" Not exactly negative words, but not what Rose had expected.

Because the words were written, Rose had no way to know the expression or emotion that went along with the comments on the paper. If her teacher had been orally critiquing her work, Mrs. Gambert could have said, "You have nice handwriting!" Rose would have felt encouraged. Or she could have said, "Well, you have nice handwriting . . . ," leaving Rose to wonder what the rest of that sentence was. Or Mrs. Gambert could have said, "You really have nice handwriting!"

Because it was written on paper, Rose was left to add the emotion herself and interpret it as she saw fit. Because Rose has a melancholy personality, that statement was anything but positive to her. She was hoping for words of encouragement and affirmation, something that said, "Keep going. You are going to be a wonderful writer. In fact, you are well on your way!"

THE BASICS OF COMMUNICATING

Words on paper are not the same as those that are spoken. Rose found that out quickly from Mrs. Gambert. The opposite is also true. Spoken words, no matter how inspiring and wonderful, do not automatically make a book! A dynamic speaker has expertise to share. He or she wouldn't speak if that were not the case. But no matter how dynamic a speech, a speaker can't just transcribe it and produce articles or books. It takes work to make spoken words suitable for a reader.

SPEAKING VERSUS WRITING

Every culture in the world communicates in some way, most through some form of spoken language.

Talk to any parent of a toddler and you'll find that even though the child does not yet know many words, he or she is able to communicate needs to the parents.

Chrissie's mother came over to help her clean out a few closets.

Chrissie's son, Robert, toddled along after them. At one point, Robert began to cry. "I'll go change him," Chrissie's mother said.

"He's probably not wet," said Chrissie. "That's his hungry cry." Chrissie fixed him a snack and Robert was good to go for a while longer. Robert did not yet know the words to communicate his hunger, but his mother understood quite well the difference in his cries.

Have you ever been introduced to someone from another country? You felt a language barrier for sure. But before long you and your new friend found you could communicate with gestures and fragments of words.

Since many writers are speakers and many speakers are writers, it's helpful to understand the differences in verbal speech and written communication.

While speaking is usually a fast-paced activity, writing is much slower. The speed of the speech is sometimes relevant to the excitement of the speaker. Writing can be done at whatever pace the writer chooses. Speakers often speak without putting much thought into their words; writers can take time to organize their thoughts and rewrite as necessary. The detriment in that slower pace for writers is that sometimes they get bogged down in one area or they spend too much time on one chapter or one aspect of their writing.

Speakers receive immediate gratification through applause and can be encouraged by the response of their audiences through nods, laughter, and gasps. Response to writing is often slow or nonexistent.

Sharla wrote a book she knew had tremendous potential. But she became discouraged because she never heard from any reader about whether or not he or she liked the book. About three years after publication, she received a letter from a gentleman who lived halfway across the country from Sharla.

"I read your book. I was so excited I took it to the school where my children attend. I went to the school librarian and told her we needed to get that book in the library.

"But the more I thought about it," he continued, "I felt like every parent in the school needed one of those books. So I contacted the PTO to make sure they encouraged parents to read the book."

Now that was a letter worth waiting for, wouldn't you agree?

Speakers have the benefit of body language, facial expression, rhythm, and emotion. Writers must rely on punctuation and the arrangement of words to convey their messages.

When you are delivering a speech, you have the ability to change directions at the last minute. If you feel the Holy Spirit leading you to insert a special story you hadn't thought of, no problem. When you are writing a book, you edit and rewrite and edit some more until you feel as if you've done the best job you can. Then you send the finished manuscript to the publisher and you can no longer add or change anything major.

Speakers can know a little bit about their audiences before they arrive to speak. Writers have a target audience for their work, but never really know who might become one of their readers.

God has called you to be a writer; but you may find that as you begin to publish, opportunities to speak will come your way. God will equip you to communicate clearly in your area of influence. As a speaker, your area of influence is limited to the audience you have at any given time. As a writer, your area can include the entire world. Publications and books can be mailed or sent over the Internet to places you will never visit.

Effective communication doesn't come easily for many people. But you can develop your communication skills to impart the message God has given you clearly and concisely.

"Your communication will reveal the kind of person you really are, because what comes out of your mouth is usually what's in your heart. If you truly desire to exemplify Christ, you will seek to become a good communicator. Everything Jesus Christ communicated was holy, clear, purposeful, and timely."

—STUART SCOTT, THE EXEMPLARY HUSBAND

 PLAN

Many writers just sit down and begin to create a talk or book. But the key to effective communication is planning. For the organized people who are reading this, planning translates to outlining. An effective outline can help you stay on track and focus on your topic. The better and more thorough your outline, the easier it will be when the time to deliver your message comes, whether verbally or written.

Josie wrote her first book several years ago and has had a prolific writing career since she started. She says, "For my first book I had a 35-page outline." She laughs. "I know that sounds excessive. But because I had worked so hard on the outline, when it came time to write it was pretty easy. I knew exactly which story went where, when I had covered all I wanted to say in a chapter, and which discussion questions to include. I highly recommend a good outline!"

An outline doesn't have to be 35 pages to be effective. Start small. Break your work down into three or five major areas. Then begin filling in the gaps with your stories and essential points. You could also start with a point or word per chapter and fill in from there. Find a system that works for you and stick with it.

"From the time I knew I was going to write this book," Josie says, "I kept a folder filled with information on the subject. I didn't even bother to organize it very well. But once I created my outline, it was easy to go back and plug all the information into the proper chapter."

Once you write a book, you have plenty of well-organized material from which to create a talk. Likewise, if you have prepared a speech and it is well organized, it could become a chapter of your book. In this planning stage, make sure you save all your research. You never know when you may need to go back and flesh out a subject.

> *A truly wise person uses few words; a person with understanding is even-tempered.*
>
> PROVERBS 17:27

 PERSEVERE

It probably sounds like a lot of work to be a writer. It is. But when you've been called to be a writer for the kingdom of God, you can do nothing else if you want to be obedient to God and follow His plan for your life.

You must persevere. At times it feels like an impossible task to complete an entire book or even an article. Writers are busy people and life continues despite deadlines.

Margit has been a writer for years. She has raised three children during her writing career. "At times it was really hard. I wrote every spare minute. But the spare minutes were sparse. And if my writing started flowing, I often had to stop to kiss a boo-boo, cook dinner, referee an altercation, or look at a new rock. It was hard to do that cheerfully. But I knew God understood those interruptions and I had to be true to my primary calling of wife and mother. God never failed to redeem any time I took away from my writing to serve my family."

If you are overwhelmed by a project, try compartmentalizing it. An entire book does seem a lot to accomplish. But could you just do one chapter? Or if that feels overwhelming, concentrate on just one section or just doing research for one section. You obviously have an interest in the subject or you wouldn't have started a book. Pray before you start and ask God to give you the strength to stick with the project and to point you to the wisdom you need to create a dynamite book.

If you are really struggling, you may need to reassess your decision to write a book. Do you really have enough information to write an entire book? Maybe you need to write a series of articles instead. Perhaps writing a series of articles will inspire and excite you all over again about your subject and then you will be ready to write an entire book.

 ## PERFECT

This is not the adjective, but the verb *perfect*. In this case it refers to writing, editing, and rewriting your information until it is the best it can possibly be. This feels tedious, but this is what is going to make your manuscript stand out from all the rest.

Get your checklist and go over it one last time to make sure you have done exactly what the publisher asked for. If you have a contract for your book, ask for a style sheet to make sure your writing fits the wishes of the publisher. Be diligent about staying within word count and adjusting margins. If the guidelines say no special formatting such as bold, italics, or all caps, delete any that you may have used. Now is the time to let those perfectionist tendencies shine!

 ## PRESENT

Presenting a manuscript to a publisher is exciting. You have the opportunity to share your passion with someone who can open the door to the world. Your message is important. You are a writer on mission for God and you want to present the best product you have to accomplish your mission.

What does that mean? For one thing it means you have completed the previous step. Everything about your work is as good as you can possibly make it. You have edited and possibly even hired an editor to edit for you. Some people may wonder why that is even a suggestion. After all, haven't you already edited and edited and edited again?

Yes, you have. But you only have one chance to make a good first impression; and if you send a manuscript needing lots of editorial work, that translates into dollar signs for a publisher. One of the first things the publisher looks at is what his or her investment in this book will have to be. Spending money to hire an editor is money well spent. You may not think you will recoup that with your first book, but the money is an investment in your career. Making a good first impression will pay off later.

Be sure to obtain guidelines from the publisher or magazine you are pitching to. Nothing is more embarrassing than presenting something to a professional that their guidelines clearly says they do not accept. The editor won't forget that mistake and you probably won't either.

 PRAY

Prayer should be at the top of the list. Your work should start with prayer. Before you ever write a word, you should ask God's blessing and guidance on your work. At the start of your work would be a good time to enlist several close friends as your project prayer team. Find a few people who will commit to praying for you throughout the project and who will keep you accountable.

Louise organized her prayer team when she began writing her first book. She carefully chose people she knew would be faithful to pray. She sent a note periodically that listed the projects she was working on, places she was speaking, and specific prayer requests. Throughout the writing of her books—that one and everyone thereafter—she received notes of encouragement and emailed prayers, and one of her prayer team even brought an ice-cream cone to let her know she was praying.

The entire book or article should be bathed in prayer. Pray every morning before you begin your work. Pray throughout when you question whether or not to include certain information or quotes. At the end of the day thank God if it's been a productive day and ask for His blessing on the next.

Darlene prayed often during her last book project. "There were times I really struggled," she said. "In fact, I remember one time when I felt like I was done. But I was 15,000 words short! At the end of the day I had to just say, 'God, I have said everything I possibly can about this subject. If there is more You want me to write, You are going to have to give me the words.' And He did!"

End your project with a prayer of thanksgiving for God's blessing and guidance on your work. You want to submit a stellar piece any time you send something to an editor. Submit your work literally on the wings of a prayer.

That may sound strange not to suggest a prayer for publication. However, if you are a writer on mission, and God has told you to write a book, you have completed your mission with the last word of the book. It is up to Him to take it and use it and open doors for your message to go out and change the world.

Finish that book, lift it up to Him as an offering, and then step back and watch what happens. Be ready to do everything you can to make that book a success, but realize the legwork is up to you; the outcome is up to God.

May the words of my mouth and the thoughts of my heart be pleasing to you, O Lord, my rock and my redeemer.

PSALM 19:14

No matter where you are or what you say or do, people are watching and you are sending a message with your life. As Paul reminded us in the verse that began this chapter, even if you never put another word on paper, you're sharing a message with the world. Your relationship with God dictates the message people will read through your life. Will it be a positive word that points them to Jesus?

THE MISSIONARY IN YOU

1. Do you realize when you have been called as a writer on mission your calling is just as important as the missionary who physically moves his family around the world to tell others about Jesus? What affirmation do you have of that?

2. Being able to continue to write and tell others about Jesus is dependent on your relationship with Him. What is your favorite way of spending time with Him?

3. Madeline often takes time from her writing and declares a "Jesus and me" day for personal refreshment. What do you do to "recharge" your batteries?

4. When you develop your prayer team, be sure to include your readers on the list of things to pray for. Whom do you see as your target audience for your current project?

THE WRITER IN YOU

1. When we sit at our computers all day, we don't necessarily feel like missionaries. What do you do to stay focused on your mission?

2. What do you do when you feel you have run out of words?

3. Are you comfortable using outlines? If not, commit to using an outline for your next writing project no matter how hard it may seem to do that. As you use outlines, you will find it becomes easier. You will also find that as you learn to use an outline, your work will become more organized and efficient.

4. Paul reminded us that we are living a message with our lives even if we don't write. What is your message and how can you best communicate that in writing?

A WRITER'S PRAYER

Dear God, I want the message people are reading with my life to be exactly what You intend it to be. Fill me with Your love. Draw me closer to You each day. Make my life a billboard that makes people want to get to know You. Oh, dear God, I love You so much. Amen.

The Basics of Communicating to Reach Others

HEART TO HEART—HOW TO KNOW
AND REACH YOUR AUDIENCE

But in your hearts set apart Christ as Lord. Always be prepared to give an answer to everyone who asks you to give the reason for the hope that you have. But do this with gentleness and respect.

1 PETER 3:15

Y ou are a writer on mission. What is your mission? Your mission simply defined is to communicate the truth of Jesus Christ to a world that desperately needs to hear it. Sounds fairly simple, right? Simple if you have the right tools. You wouldn't want any professional working *for* you or *on* you unless they had the right training and tools, would you?

A recent television commercial portrays a man walking into his kitchen where the plumber is under the sink fixing the plumbing. When he hears footsteps, the plumber sticks his head out and smiles.

The man looks puzzled and says, "Hey, don't I know you?"

The plumber says, "Yeah, we met last week."

The man replies, "That was when I got my taxes prepared. You said you were an expert tax preparer."

"Yep, I sure am. That was last week. This week I am a master plumber."

The point of the commercial is that the man under the sink maybe knows a little about a lot of things but is not really an expert in anything; and if you want things done right, you should consult an expert. The commercial goes on to advertise where you can find an expert.

God has made you an expert in the area of your life experience and your relationship with Him. If you know Him and have spent time building a relationship with Him, you have a message the world needs to hear. God calls people to share their messages, personal testimonies, in many different ways. If you are reading this book, God has called you to be a writer on mission, a writer to communicate His message of hope with a lost world.

HOW TO COMMUNICATE AS A WRITER ON MISSION

To be the most effective writer possible, you must learn and practice the techniques of good writing. No, you must practice the techniques of excellent writing. God gave His best for us; we should do no less.

Writing with excellence to accomplish your mission requires studying, mastering writing tools and techniques, and hard work. To communicate with clear truth, you must use the best mechanics of writing, contemporary style, and grammar the world understands. You are communicating the message of heaven. You take the truth of the Bible, take it to heart, and put it in words the world will understand. You are a translator translating the language of heaven into the language of the world.

STYLE

As your writing career progresses, you will develop a personal and recognizable style of writing. Style encompasses many things. When you prepare to write books for a publishing house or magazine articles for a periodical, it is beneficial to request a style sheet. Or you can make your own by studying their previous publications. Here are some things to look for.

SUBHEADS. Do chapters or articles have subheads? If so, how many in a chapter, or how many words per subhead?

BULLET POINTS. Do they use bullets or numbering for lists, or do they list with no identifying marks at all?

BIBLE TRANSLATION. Is there a certain translation of the Bible that the publisher prefers?

LENGTH. Most publishing houses have a preferred length of their books or articles.

FONT STYLES. Most publishers prefer sparse or no use of bold, italics, and underlined type. When their staff begins to work on the piece, they must first remove all formatting and style. If you think a particular style is needed, make a note to the editor/designer.

You will soon develop your own style. You'll have a favorite translation of the Bible, you'll see places that just beg for bullets, and you'll find that most of your chapters or articles are close to the same length. If you question what your style is, look at your writing port-folio. Examine your early writing and then compare it with today's writing. Of course, you'll see improvement, but you'll also see your personal style develop. Remember, however, when you are writing on assignment to consider carefully the style of your assigning editor.

 GRAMMAR

"That is mine toy!" Brad yelled.

"Brad, it is *my* toy, not *mine* toy," his mom replied.

"No, it's mine toy," Brad said again.

"My toy. I was trying to help you learn the right word. I know it is not my toy!"

Brad's mother smiled. When she thought about the complexity of the language and how articulate and fluent her toddlers were, she marveled at how she had watched their language skills develop.

Brad shows you how important using the correct pronouns is. One little mix-up of a word and the context of whose toy it is has totally changed.

Grammar is the way sentences are constructed and every language has set rules for that. Using good grammar not only indicates that you know the language and have a good command of its usage, but good grammar also allows you to communicate clearly and understandably.

PUNCTUATION

Grammar's partner in helping you communicate clearly and concisely is punctuation.

Punctuation is a series of marks such as a comma, period, semicolon, colon, question mark, parentheses, etc., that helps you communicate the context and meaning of your writing. Unlike verbal communication, where you have the benefit of body language and facial expression as well as voice inflection, written communication needs punctuation to indicate when a sentence is finished, to show where the writer pauses, to indicate when he or she asks a question, and to keep words from having multiple meanings.

Look at this sentence. See what a difference punctuation makes?

- A woman without her man is nothing.
- A woman without her man, is nothing.
- A woman, without her, man is nothing.

Here's another one. One little comma saved Mom's life!

- "I'm starving. Let's eat Mom," said David.
- "I'm starving. Let's eat, Mom," said David.

W WORDS

Oh, the power of words. Words can encourage, words can build up and edify, or words can change an otherwise gloomy day into one full of sunshine. At the same time words can hurt, discourage, destroy, and ruin an otherwise perfectly good day.

We need to choose our words carefully. Beyond that, we need to place them carefully on the page once we have chosen them.

For example, a recent news story stated, "The injured dog was discovered by an oilfield worker wrapped in a towel inside a white trash bag." The misplaced phrase makes you think this oil worker has extremely unusual tastes in attire.

The clearer way to write that would be, "An oilfield worker discovered an injured dog wrapped in a towel inside a white trash bag."

The first way of reporting that incident is also passive voice which is something writers need to use sparingly. See how much stronger the sentence is when it is written in active voice?

Speaking of active and passive voice, if you have a choice whether or not to use active voice, always choose active voice. It will make your writing much stronger and make it come alive. Storytellers sometimes slip into passive when they are recounting a story. But if you can bring your storytelling into the present, it will make a lasting impression.

Writers sometimes have a hard time understanding the difference in passive voice and active voice. Some writers even switch back and forth, causing great confusion for their readers. When grammar school teachers teach grammar, I don't think students realize what a lifelong lesson they are learning. Obviously from what we read today some students didn't pay a lot of attention in grammar class. I hope the few reminders here will bring back to mind all your early grammar lessons!

The thing to remember with active and passive voice is not too hard to remember.

ACTIVE: The subject is performing the action.
PASSIVE: The subject is the object of the action of someone or something else.

PASSIVE: The cake batter was mixed by Mary Ann.
ACTIVE: Mary Ann mixed the cake batter.

PASSIVE: A great sermon was preached by the pastor.
ACTIVE: The pastor preached a great sermon.

PASSIVE: Attacks on the minister of youth's integrity were made by members of the church leadership.
ACTIVE: Members of the church leadership attacked the minister of youth's integrity.

From these examples you can see how much stronger and clearer the active voice is. The passive voice is usually wordy and much harder to read and understand.

Some words are commonly confused. Writers need to know what those words are and make sure they use them correctly. Many of them are *homophones,* and when they are spoken, the ear hears the correct word and the mind translates into the correct form of the word. However, when we write our thoughts, using a word that sounds like what we want to say but is spelled differently cannot only change the meaning of the sentence but also can make us look as if we haven't done out homework and learned our lessons well.

Some of the most commonly confused words are:

- *There*—a place. This indicates location.
  She put the book there.
- *They're*—a contraction. The shortened form of *they are*.
  They're home from vacation.
- *Their*—possessive form of *they*.
  Singers often clear their voices.

- *Who*—used as a subject.
  Who left the cap off the toothpaste?
- *Whom*—used as the object.
  Whom did the pastor choose for the leader of the finance committee?

- *A lot*—two words that mean *many*.
  A lot of people watched the race.
- *Alot*—Not a word.

- *To*—movement meaning *toward*.
  Janet went to the store.
- *Two*—a number.
  Janet bought two apples at the store.
- *Too*—*also* or *in addition to*; can also mean *excessively*.
  Janet went to the bank too.

- *Affect*—*to influence*.
  Insomnia affects your performance at work.
- *Effect*—*result*.
  The lasting effects of the flu are difficult to shake.

Clichés are another often misused and too frequently used form of writing. What is a cliché? A cliché is a phrase or series of words that have been used over and over again that bring an immediate thought or picture to mind. Instead of using a cliché, why not come up with a new fresh way to say something? Find a new way of expressing your thoughts that could make your reader stop and think—and probably smile at the same time.

A few of the most common clichés are:

- Quiet as a mouse.
- My ox is in the ditch.
- In a nutshell.
- Float your boat.
- Out of the box.
- Silence is golden.
- Let the cat out of the bag.
- Salt of the earth.
- Wrong side of the bed.
- Two peas in a pod.

Avoiding the expressions above—and quite a few more—is part of self-editing, an important step in your writing process. You don't want any extra words in your writing. You do not want to use more passive voice than absolutely necessary. When you finish a manuscript, it often helps to read your work aloud. You will detect mistakes you might otherwise miss.

"When I read aloud, my ear catches what my eye misses."
—CECIL MURPHEY

 GENRES

To reiterate, your readers are unique individuals. As we strive to understand how to reach them by understanding their personalities, we also need to understand their reading preferences. As writers, different genres provide varied ways to reach your readers.

What is a *genre*? That word is even difficult to say. Practice "ZHAHN-rah." Not so easy to roll off the tongue but an important word in the writing world. *Merriam-Webster's Collegiate Dictionary*, 11th Edition, defines *genre* as "a category of artistic, musical, or literary composition characterized by a particular style, form, or content."

The writing world has many genres with new ones popping up occasionally. Both fiction and nonfiction have a number of genres and most readers find a few from the list that are their favorites.

FICTION GENRES

Fiction contains many genres and subgenres. We will discuss a few of the most popular. When you learn what they are, you'll see why one or the other appeals to you and another to someone else. Because of the differences in our personalities, we are drawn to a certain type of story.

Novels of today fall into many categories. Some you may be familiar with. Some you may want to explore. All are tools God can use to bring others to Him. If you are a Christian fiction writer, please don't ever think you are just entertaining your readers. Every word you write, every story you tell should subtly and gently point your readers to the Father. Even though you may be writing stories that are only real in your mind and the minds of your readers, you have the opportunity to point readers to the truth. Don't miss those opportunities.

FLASH FICTION—A story that is told in 1,000 words or less. This is becoming more popular today as readers want to spend less and less time reading. They like something they can finish quickly.

ADVENTURE FICTION—Stories with characters who experience a lot of dangerous or adventurous action.

ALLEGORY—Stories that use symbolism to impart truth. One of the most famous allegories is John Bunyan's *The Pilgrim's Progress*.

CRIME OR DETECTIVE FICTION—Fiction based on crime and the investigation of wrongdoing.

EPIC FICTION—Originally you heard the word *epic* more often associated with poetry. Now, long prose that exploits a factual or fictitious hero is also considered epic.

FANTASY FICTION—Stories that involve imaginary characters. Can be set in a real world or an imaginary one. These stories often contain magic or characters with supernatural powers.

ROMANCE—Love stories. This genre has many subgenres. History enthusiasts can enjoy historical fiction. Other categories are contemporary romance, inspirational romance, and multicultural romance. Romantic suspense combines mystery with love.

SCIENCE FICTION, OFTEN CALLED SCI-FI—This genre relies on science and technology as important parts of the stories. Possibly set in the future or on other planets.

These are only a few of the fiction subgenres.

NONFICTION GENRES

BIOGRAPHY—The true story of one person's life. You have been familiar with biographies since grade school. Reading what others have accomplished and hurdles they have overcome is inspirational.

ESSAY—An article or book that reflects the viewpoint of the author. Opinion pieces are similar and popular with readers. Included in this genre are memoirs, travel pieces, and personal essays.

NARRATIVE—Facts told through story. Also known as creative nonfiction. Employs the use of fiction elements to present truth in story form. Subgenres in this category include devotions, profiles, personal experience, and more.

Christian writers have a tremendous honor and responsibility as communicators of the gospel. God has called writers to join the saints and apostles as those who impart truth to readers. Writers are given the opportunity to live out the Great Commission without ever leaving their desks. Being called to be a Great Commission writer keeps you on your toes (oops, a cliché here!) and on your knees. Unless you are very secure in your relationship with God, you cannot express to others the need to get to know Him and remain in close fellowship.

"Our lives begin to end the day we become silent about things that matter."
—MARTIN LUTHER KING JR.

THE MISSIONARY IN YOU
1. Do you wake up each morning thinking about those who will read your words?
2. Do you pray that your readers will "hear" clearly the message you have written?
3. When writing, does it really excite you to feel the words flowing from you because you know it is the Holy Spirit directing you?
4. When you are overwhelmed by the calling to be God's print messenger, what do you do? Stop and communicate with the Father until you feel ready to write again.

THE WRITER IN YOU

1. Writing is such a blessing but some days it doesn't feel so easy. Clear communication can be hard even when you follow the rules of good communication. Pray every day before you start your work that God will use you to communicate truth to your readers.

2. Remember the teacher who taught you grammar? Take time to write him or her a note of thanks.

3. Think of one person you haven't seen in five years or more. Ask God to help you reconnect through Facebook or one of the other social media. Share a word of encouragement with him or her.

4. Perhaps there is a family relationship that is a bit tense at the moment. Ask God to help you diffuse that tension. Write a note to your family member heralding the blessing of family and your desire to be closer to him or her.

A WRITER'S PRAYER

God, You communicated Your love to us in such a magnificent way when You sent Your Son Jesus to die for us. Thank You. Make us faithful to the task of telling the world about Him. Thank You for Your written Word that we can go to daily to learn and grow in You. Amen.

Ministry: The Servant in a Writer on Mission:

WRITING AS A MINISTRY—THE SERVING STAGE OF WRITING FOR CHRIST

I write these things to you who believe in the name of the Son of God so that you may know that you have eternal life in his name.

1 JOHN 5:13

"Brrrrring!"

Sitting at her desk at home working on an urgent book deadline, Phyllis hesitated to answer the phone since she didn't want to waste time talking. In a few minutes, she realized this was one of the most important phone calls she could ever answer. Heather, a women's ministry director on the other end of the line, would change Phyllis's life.

"Thank heavens I reached you," she said.

Phyllis was listening halfheartedly, glancing at the screen and correcting a typo. "I just wanted you to know you saved a church from closing its doors."

"What?" Phyllis stopped looking at her manuscript and pressed the receiver closer.

"It started last year," Heather said. "I was a new women's ministry leader at this church, and as soon as I moved into my office, a member named Sue told me of trouble between her and an anonymous churchwoman. The next day a second woman, Janie, came in to complain about her aunt and other family members in our church. I listened, trying to give each woman wise counsel."

"How does that involve me?" Phyllis asked, looking at her manuscript waiting on the screen at her desk.

"We had begun several new women's Bible studies on Wednesday nights. On a staggered schedule, five groups started different studies—some with videos, some with books. . . . Two of the groups were studying your book on Philippians."

Heather told Phyllis how well the five studies had progressed, with no complaints from anyone except these two women, unrelated to the Bible study groups. "I had hoped the Bible studies would help women get back to basics and let Christ lead them through their problems and find hope."

Meanwhile, she explained, the church had bigger problems. Factions of the church seemed at warfare against one another, some even fighting among their own families over who had authority to make church decisions. Then one day Sue and Janie showed up in Heather's office at the same time. Surprised, she found they knew each other. Sue had reported Janie anonymously for harassing her, and Janie's family problem was Sue, her aunt! Both women had come to Heather to ask for forgiveness.

Heather explained to Phyllis, the Philippians Bible study author:

> In the first chapter of your book, Sue and Janie—each
> in a separate study group—had explored Philippians
> I, where Paul confesses he and Timothy are "servants
> of Christ," and, along with their separate groups, Sue
> and Janie had learned the art of "under-ing"—that is,
> staying *under* the leadership of Jesus. Neither of them

knew the written word was profoundly affecting
the other to recognize the authority of Christ. Janie
was particularly hard hit by the words about fathers
saying, "Do this *because I said so*." Her father agreed
with her aunt Sue on the church's controversies, and
Janie realized she had a problem with authority—not
only that of her father—a deacon in the church—but
also the authority of her heavenly Father. She decided
to serve *Him* because *He* said so.

Meanwhile, Sue had felt the Holy Spirit speaking to her. In chapter
2, she read reverently as Paul called the Philippians "saints" (v. 2) led
by "overseers and deacons." The Holy Spirit touched both women,
who realized they hadn't come under *Christ's authority*, instead siding
with opposing leaders in their church! With tears, Sue and Janie
asked for forgiveness and pledged to help the church cooperate
rather than fight with one another. Transformed, these two women
left Heather's office determined to change the church one member
at a time. Today the church has grown spiritually and physically,
with a new spirit sweeping across all the members, initiated by the
women in the Bible study groups.

"If it hadn't been for your book's chapter on authority," said
Heather, "our church would be closing its doors and dividing the
property. With the Holy Spirit, it took only two women to change
our church."

After Phyllis hung up, she thanked God that He had used her
words in this women's ministry. She stopped and remembered how
stressed she had been when she wrote the Philippians book. She
had finished it in a sweaty room with a broken air-conditioning
system on the hottest day of that year (102 degrees!). Phyllis had
been so eager to send it to the publisher that she had barely looked
at it before sending it off. She says, "I totally forgot the power

of a Christian's Spirit-filled words. I never imagined my words would be significant to two women a year later in another church, in another region! My words—God's words filtered through my spirit and mind and then recorded on my computer—came alive in a ministry to two women who had failed to recognize their allegiance to Christ. Once they tried the art of under-ing, willingly submitting under His authority, they changed their world!

WRITING AS A MINISTRY OF A WRITER ON MISSION

Christian writer, you are holding tremendous power in your words as you submit to the authority of Christ. Your writing is a ministry to others who desperately need to hear Him through you.

In the first ten chapters of this book, you have studied how your spirituality leads to Scripture study, which changes your worldview. Once you have a Christian worldview, you see opportunities to share that worldview through all your relationships. As you mature as a Christian, you seek to communicate the gospel, not only through all your relationships but also through a ministry. As you mature in Christ, you want to serve God as He calls you into specific ministry toward others you may not even know!

You hold in your hands, your heart, your head—and even your fingertips—the power of ministry through the written word. Ministry is considered the act of helping, sharing, or bettering the lives of others to bring them happiness, ease, or beneficial conditions. As John says in the Scripture verse at the beginning of this chapter, he intended the words he wrote to help readers believe that Jesus was the "Christ, the Son of God, and that believing [they] may have life in his name." As Christians, we get involved with social issues such as poverty, disease, crime, illiteracy, human trafficking, or other causes of pain in people, just as non-Christians get involved out of pity for suffering people, but with the added component of Christian ministry: sharing the hope humans find in Christ.

How can you communicate hope through a writing ministry?

 PROFESSOR

First, you minister as a *word professor*. In general, Christians communicate the gospel through television or street evangelism, community Bible studies, a local pastor's preaching and counseling, Scripture distribution, or missionary service to special people groups— nearby or overseas. They are word professors, professing Christ using many methods in many places. Each of these settings involves writers, once they feel a call from God to a writing ministry.

Jenna, a college sophomore, saw Christian writing as a simple form of communicating the gospel. Period. She failed to see the myriad forms of writing as *ministry*, not just communication. One day as she prayed, she answered the call to be a word professor.

You don't have to be a college instructor to be a professor. You can profess the gospel by writing alone in a torn T-shirt and jeans, in a semidark room at your desk, just as well as a spotlighted evangelist

FORMS OF WORD-PROFESSOR MINISTRY

The following are only a few of the ways God leads writers to share the gospel:

- Witnessing leaflets with the plan of salvation
- Scripture portions in small booklets
- Take-home leaflets for children of all ages
- Scholarly Bible commentaries
- Scripture translations with annotations
- Magazine articles
- Bible study books
- Books on Christian living
- Personal memoirs
- Blogs
- Letters to your grand-children
- How-to books
- Textbooks for seminaries
- Manuals for mission service
- Christian songs on sheet music or songbooks
- Music or sermons on CDs, DVDs, or live streaming
- Christian poetry as a side-bar or a collection

OTHER WRITING MINISTRIES:

- Movie scripts
- Art design
- Electronic visuals using words of all kinds
- Managing a publishing house
- Editing and proofreading

in a sharp, gray suit in a stadium before thousands of people. God uses both the written and spoken word. In 1 Timothy 6:12, Paul calls young Timothy to "fight the good fight" because he has already "professed a good profession before many witnesses."

Most writers also are speakers, explaining their books or articles, which have created a platform for their spoken words. You may be a writer who speaks or a speaker who writes. Either way, whether you're speaking as a church leader or writing your life's verses for your grandchildren to read someday, God can use your efforts to bless the world as a word professor.

Y YOURSELF

As a writer on mission, you sometimes minister to yourself. For years, people have used writing as therapy. Those with psychological problems find catharsis in writing about their fears, the past, or dreams of the future. No doubt the average writers find some catharsis in their writing, but it offers many other benefits. God ministers to us through others' accolades, invitations, royalties from a publisher, or words of praise from readers. Nothing blesses us like a child who says, "Wow! Thanks for the kind words. I love you," or "Oh, Mom, I've enjoyed this sweet card made just for me. What a memory of your wedding day! I never knew that."

While few Christian authors write just for the monetary benefits, they admit God blesses them as a side benefit to their writing. As stated in an earlier chapter of this book, your Christ-centered worldview influences the way you think about money and making a living as a writer. God says in Hebrews 13:5, "Keep your lives free from the love of money and be content with what you have." He promises to take care of all our needs.

After spending hundreds of dollars on a writers conference, a Christian writer said, "Isn't it great God allows us to go broke writing for Him?" He ministers to Christian writers, even if

remuneration doesn't pay the bills or recognition doesn't bring
fame. If God calls us as Holy Word professors, we're grateful for
a pat on the head. We eagerly await a "Well done, [my] good and
faithful servant" in heaven (Luke 19:17). When ministers pour
themselves out in humility before God, the presence of the Father
brings joy that money can't buy.

R RESERVOIR

As a writer on mission you minister to others as a reservoir of
Christian principles and ideas. Excellent writing requires research.
Most Bible teachers recognize they learn more than anyone in
their classes. If you love to write, you're probably a good reservoir
for random Christian facts. Studying for one Christian topic may
teach you trivia about other topics. One writer complained,

> My family and my church family come to me as the
> office of record for every fact in the world! They
> think that because I've written one book, I know
> everything! Thank goodness for the Internet. I look
> their question up, zip them an answer, and they think
> I'm a genius. I'm glad I can help . . . I think.

Research helps us learn everything about everything, as we spend
time with Jesus and His Word. Think of it as a lifetime of filling
of your inner spirit, a reservoir, which pours out through the
Holy Spirit into your writing. How do you get this ability to be
His reservoir? Ask for it. Jesus tells us to keep on asking, keep on
seeking, and keep on knocking on His door (Luke 11:9).

John describes what happened when Jesus called His first
disciples: "They said, . . . 'where are you staying?' 'Come,' he replied,
'and you will see.' So they went and saw where he was staying, and
spent that day with him" (John 1:38–39). Over and over in New

Testament Scriptures we find disciples coming from everywhere, dropping their fishing nets, their plows, or their tax money and *following* Him so they can *spend time* with Him. Every moment you spend with Him fills your reservoir. You can splash that living water onto others only as you spend time with Him to fill that reservoir to overflowing.

H HURTING

A writer on mission also ministers to hurting souls. Why do you recommend books to others? To heal their souls. You can alleviate pain on earth through sharing what you know about heaven. Your writing ministry is not about you; God speaks *through your written words* to minister to hurting individuals.

> *You can alleviate pain on earth through sharing what you know about heaven.*

When you write, don't address a plural audience. Remember, you're speaking to one reader at a time. It's all right to speak to the second person, *you*, your reader, in a conversational tone (not your *readers*, plural). God's Spirit heals people one heart at a time. Your book on overcoming cancer can give hope to a cancer patient. Your magazine article on mental illness or stress (back copies you've ordered free after the publication month is over) can encourage someone for years as a handy cherished display on the coffee table.

W WRITERS

A writer on mission also writes as a ministry to other writers. He or she can teach at a writers conference, mentor one-on-one at the kitchen table, form a critique group in the neighborhood, or start a group of writers at church to write devotions for Lent before Easter or Advent before Christmas.

One of the greatest ministries for a writer benefits children at a local school. On Arts Day or Book Emphasis Day at the high school, middle school, or elementary school, you can show children that they, too, can become writers like you. Set up a book table with your biographies, picture books, pamphlets, compilation devotions, cookbooks, short stories, or other writings and sell the items to pass along the message to another generation. Children are often amazed to learn they can become productive writers. Someone needs to tell them the facts in a realistic way. You might be that someone who makes a difference in their lives as they begin writing as future writers on mission.

However you write as a ministry, whether you minister to children, teens or adults, men or women, you can help heal hearts and souls. AIDS, anti-immune diseases, autism, and other medical or social issues on the forefront of the news make you want to minister. Ask God to guide you to an up-and-running organization or media publisher for whom you can write to minister to more people. Think of volunteering as an *avocation* and a writing career as a *vocation* at a large ministry organization. If you are dissatisfied

EDITOR TIPS TO PASS ALONG TO OTHERS

- Never write, "Between you and I." (It's always "between you and me.")

- Don't indent the first line underneath a headline or subheadline. (Indent all other paragraphs.)

- Don't use block style (Normal) unless your publisher requires it.

- Use only one space at the end of sentences. (Forget the old two-spaces rule.)

- Show; don't tell. "She turned pale. Her palms sweated," instead of "She looked nervous."

"He hopped on one foot, with his car keys in his mouth, jerking his sock on with one hand and pulling up his pants with the other," instead of "He was not ready."

with other ministries or haven't found a ministry that suits your writing gifts, start your own.

THE MISSIONARY IN YOU

1. Have you had a similar experience to that of Phyllis, when her church experienced friction among members because of an authority issue? How can you help if you're ever in that situation again?
2. How can you teach others the art of under-ing?
3. For which of the ministries listed in the first sidebar do you have a passion?
4. How is God nudging you to share the gospel through your passion for this ministry?
5. How much time can you make to *spend the day with Jesus*? Tell others how they can do the same.

EDITOR TIPS (continued)

- Eliminate the following, when possible:
  adverbs (seemingly, ordinarily, hopefully, very); adjectives (happy, nice); slang (wanna, way—as in way loved or way high in the sky or way wrong); the verb to be: am, is, was, were, be, being, been.

Examples:
Wrong / *Correct*

I was walking alone. I wandered alone./*I tiptoed alone.*

There were three men who were on the corner./ *Three men danced on the corner.*

I had been helped. The song was sung. / *She helped me. He sang the song.*

He is at school / *He learns at school.*

THE WRITER IN YOU

1. Have you ever been tempted to write just to earn money? Is this necessarily a bad aim? When do you believe it can become a sin?
2. Which of the grammatical errors in the editor tips sidebar do you make too often? What can you do to polish your craft to become a more competent writer?
3. If your passion is to focus on telling the world about Jesus, then why is it important to write without common grammatical errors?

4. Name one hurt in your life that you've learned how to overcome. How can you help others with the same problems through the words you write?

A WRITER'S PRAYER

Help me remember, O God, that You are the Master of healing anyone and anything that hurts. O Great Physician, minister to others through my words as a Christian writer, dedicated to serve You. Help me to minister to other writers in various stages of life. Make me a better Christian servant through the exercise of writing. Come into my heart anew, Lord, and fill me to overflowing so that others can read the overflow. In Jesus' name, amen.

The Basics of Writing for Ministry

PARTNERING WITH OTHERS — HOW TO WRITE FOR MINISTERING SAINTS

Do nothing out of vain conceit, but in humility consider others better than yourselves. Each of you should look not only to your own interests but also to the interests of others.

PHILIPPIANS 2:3–4

Two missions-hearted writers drove from Spartanburg, South Carolina, to Orlando, Florida, to attend a national missions meeting. After the last session, they rode over to the coast to visit a seamen's center before heading north. They watched as two Eastern European sailors dropped in to collect a free knit cap, pick up a complimentary Bible in their own language, and make free telephone calls to their families back home.

"Someone had to write all these witnessing leaflets in various languages," Ann said. "We could write something similar to fit our area's needs."

"Yes," answered Jean. "And someone wrote these Bibles in all these languages."

"And even the instructions on these signs above the telephones."

Both women agreed the written word was important in missions and ministries to people all around the world. They examined several books, and picked up a few pamphlets with instructions on how to knit the caps, volunteer in the center, and give to the seamen's ministry.

"Women in our church can knit warm sailor caps from these written instructions."

"Sure. Let's get a few more packets. This winter we can lead lots of women in our church to donate caps to this center." In addition to the cap-instruction packets, they took a few free witnessing leaflets, "Life's Hope," to share with the Logos Writers, a critique group in their church, as a model for writing a gospel message.

An hour later the women visited a busy church center on Merritt Island they had heard about at the conference. People bustled through the food pantry, the thrift store, the library, and the clothes closet ministry. One of the volunteers showed them several men's suits that had just come in. As they examined the high-end labels inside the jackets, a volunteer insisted they take three of the suits, saying, "I'm sure someone in your church could use these." Ann and Jean couldn't think of anyone in their church in South Carolina who needed the suits, but when the volunteer insisted, they reluctantly took them. The volunteer carefully packed them in an old suitcase made of bright blue plastic and the women left for the long drive home, expecting to arrive before bedtime that evening.

Five hours later, they stopped in Savannah for dinner. When they came out of the restaurant, their car wouldn't start. After a quick visit from a roadside service, they called a wrecker to take the car to a local shop for repair the next day.

"I think God has a hand in this," said Ann.

"What? It looks like a disaster to me!"

"Jean, can't you see it? We've already had a chance to encourage the people in the restaurant, going back in several times after the car broke down, and changing their frowns to smiles. And you witnessed to the man who answered our distress call. He took that 'Hope' leaflet home with him."

"That's true. He did seem happy to take it. He said he had family troubles."

"God placed a hotel right across the street from where our car broke down, and we got a discounted price for the night!"

"Sure . . . I guess."

"And we've been able to tell the desk clerks about how we're trusting God to get us home. One of them said he was interested in going back to church next Sunday. He took one of our 'Hope' leaflets too."

"Yes. We did get a good night's rest too."

The owner of the repair shop interrupted them. "Only a few minutes till your car's ready, ma'am." He looked at one of his employees, Rob, coming in a side door.

"Bad news."

"I knew it," Jean whispered to Ann.

"I'm going to have to go home," Rob said. "My uncle died, and I don't have a suit to wear to the funeral."

"What size do you wear?" Jean smiled at Ann.

You can guess the end of the story. The man and two members of his family who worked in the shop were the exact sizes to fit the three suits in the ugly blue suitcase, which Jean was glad to get rid of. They each left with a smile and a witnessing leaflet that told them how to recover from grief by accepting the joy of Christ into their hearts.

MINISTRY OF THE WRITER ON MISSION

The world is filled with people with all kinds of social, physical, emotional, social, psychological, and other issues. Sometimes missions-minded writers can help. Hurting people surround us every day. As Christ followers, we want to help as He would but sometimes don't know how. One way to help is through the written word. If, like Jean, we fail to see opportunities, or if we can't think of a verbal response, we can write words of encouragement or other instructional words to enable those who are on the cutting edge of ministry to a hurting world. Look through the Religion section of your local newspaper or entertainment guide for worthy ministries. Go online and bring up active ministries that may need a helping hand. What a blessing a good writer would be to a ministry that is drowning in so many more needs than the present staff and volunteers can provide! Think of ways you could support hardworking ministers as you write in your community or a nearby city.

All Christian writers can make their words more valuable by determining the needs of their readers. Zero in on the passion you have for hurting people. What is a target audience you would like to help? If you consider the needs of your target audience, you can determine what kind of writing you will produce. Does a ministry near you, such as a soup kitchen, a Christian school, a mission center, or a church with ministries to the poor, need you as a volunteer writer? Do they need signs outside? Directional arrows and instructions in the hallways? Pamphlets that refer them to other social services for help? What kinds of part-time or full-time writing could you fulfill?

AREAS

Look in your area or online for the following: a formal ministry, such as a school, a homeschooling group, a denominational office, or a countywide facility. Do they need a manual for ministry? The manual will probably include an introduction with scope (a focused area of the ministry, including which age level will be helped and which area of life will be helped) and sequence (the time each segment of the ministry will take place). Sometimes a writer is asked to make a chart on a spreadsheet so a teacher or minister can see the entire program on one sheet. Often the manual will include curriculum for the ministry, with daily or weekly lessons for learners. This kind of formal ministry material will follow the ministry's mission statement (written by a writer), objectives, goals, and incremental aims (all written in a formal document by a writer), followed by an evaluation of the procedures (also designed and written by a writer).

One often-used idea for ministry is the design of informal ministry aids, which requires organic writing that just grows out of the situation, with the Holy Spirit's leadership. Look around you and see if a local situation needs someone to define the ministry and write instructional materials like the above to make a productive ministry out of chaos.

If we Christian writers identify a call from God to evangelize the world through our writing, then we need to clarify the call. Does He want us to write sermons, church staff materials, Bible studies, information for missionaries, magazine articles about the Christian life, biographies, or procedures for Sunday School lessons for children? Each of these areas is a missions field. Hurting people need many written products for ministry.

If the ministries involve immigrants or pockets of other ethnic cultures, they need writers with translation skills. You are a valuable writer if you can speak and/or read more than one language. Remember, our economical God never wastes anything. He can take the time and energy you used to learn Spanish or German in high school and use them years later in a ministry to hurting people.

> *"It is one of the ironies of the ministry that the very man who works in God's name is often hardest put to find time for God. The parents of Jesus lost Him at church, and they were not the last ones to lose Him there."*
>
> —VANCE HAVNER

If God had time to form us and equip us for ministry, we can take the time to help others in the name of Jesus.

AUDIENCE

The best way to determine what kind of writing ministry you will produce is to focus on your audience. John Vonhof had a problem with his feet, which hurt constantly. He discovered several remedies that helped his pain, and is today known as "The Feet Man." He has written hundreds of articles and pamphlets on feet. He is also a popular conference speaker. Use an Internet search engine to search for him or check out his writing ministry at fixingyourfeet.com.

Do you see a need? One man in Southern California saw hundreds of Asians pouring into his neighborhood and surrounding counties. He made friends easily, and as he talked with them, he realized they didn't understand the "crazy" Americans in this country. Even though they spoke enough English to survive in America, they were confused about this language with hundreds of idioms such as "I'm climbing the walls because of the dog's barking"; "My son's lifestyle is killing me"; "Sssssweet!"; or "He jumped out of his skin!"

Most immigrants don't understand church lingo. You might write a booklet on the rules inside churches that are *not* in the Bible or in any church bulletin. For instance, some of those unwritten, Christian-culture rules may concern dress in a church or at a gathering of church members in another place. (Choose topics you could write about from the list in the sidebar on page 163.)

Your ministry might focus on writing a sheet that answers these questions: If I've never been inside a church, what do I say or how do I act? Is it acceptable to whistle to my son to return to me and sit down? What exactly is a *pew*? Does it smell good or bad?

If I point the sole of my shoe at someone, will she be insulted as she would in my country and leave the Sunday School classroom?

Can a woman actually go into an American church unescorted by a man? Unbelievable! Do Americans really act the way I saw them in several American movies?

To which of these audiences will you minister as you write?

COMFORT WORDS

June was serving on a feeding line in Southern California after a devastating earthquake. Tired, she had already stirred huge pots of beef stew for several days, helping other volunteers feed 60,000 meals a day. A disheveled woman came by with her tray in her hand, but she stopped, saying, "I don't know who I am."

June reached across the serving table and patted the woman on the arm. "How can I help you?"

The woman put down her tray. "I've filled out so many FEMA forms today. . . . I need help for my babies, but I just don't know where to begin. I've lost my family. I've lost everything. I don't even know my name anymore. . . . I'm overwhelmed with the number of people in the shelter across the street . . . and I don't have child seats to strap my

WHICH OF THE FOLLOWING IS ACCEPTABLE INSIDE YOUR CHURCH?

- ☐ Singing (hymns, choruses, secular songs, gangsta rap)
- ☐ Gambling
- ☐ Cursing (define which slang words would or would not count as cursing)
- ☐ Scant clothing (which parts should not be exposed; churches vary in this rule)
- ☐ Smoking/using tobacco
- ☐ Praying aloud during a sermon
- ☐ Responding with an "Amen"
- ☐ Drinking wine
- ☐ Drinking beer
- ☐ Drinking mixed drinks
- ☐ Drinking tea or other caffeinated beverages
- ☐ Clapping/Applause
- ☐ Speaking in a language other than the majority's language
- ☐ Playing musical instruments (define which ones are banned from your sanctuary)
- ☐ Dancing (ballet, interpretive movement, hip-hop)
- ☐ Other: _____

children in on the vans to apply for new jobs. That will also mean more forms, and I don't think I can take another form!"

June gave her big spoon to another disaster-relief volunteer and went around to the other side of the serving line. She put her arms around the woman. "Listen to me," she said. "You're going to make it. This time the earthquake happened in your neighborhood. Next time it may happen in mine. I'm here helping you because God called me to help. If you hear of another disaster, you can help someone else next time. My name is June. I'm a mama too."

After listening to June's soothing words for a while, the woman accepted a small card from June, thanking her. Then she picked up her tray, filled it with plates and bowls of food, and returned to her children in the child-care area. At the door, she turned around and shouted. "Don't worry, June. If this ever happens to you, I'll be there to help you!"

APTLY CHOSEN

June's card read, "I will never leave you or forsake you."

June had a pile of unlined index cards, on which she had written:

> *"Cast your cares on Him, for He cares for you."*
> *"Blessed are the merciful, for they will be shown mercy."*
> *"Blessed are those who mourn, for they will be comforted."*
> *"Weeping may remain for a night, but joy comes in the morning."*
> *"Goodness and mercy shall follow me all the days of my life."*
> *"If I settle on the far side of the sea, even there Your hand will guide me."*
> *"Let us hold unswervingly to the hope we profess, for He who promised is faithful."*

Never forget the power of your words to minister to the hearts of hurting people. A few aptly chosen words can change the world.

 PRACTICE

Writers are always needed at disaster sites. They are also needed wherever there are poor, needy, confused, or hurting people. To use your words to heal others, you may want to practice by volunteering with a Christian disaster-relief agency. Many denominations have them. One can be reached at namb.net, or type *serving Christian crisis* into your Internet search engine.

 TROUBLE

What if your words don't minister? What if you have legal issues with publishers or readers because you used sensitive words you didn't realize would offend? God may call you to write about legal issues that may arise in a Christian writer's world. Or you may see that you can help confused people who need to understand churchy words, such as *salvation* or *saved, propitiation, sanctification, Calvinism, charismatic, thou, thee,* and *thine.* How about a good Christian dictionary to clarify the meanings of churchy words? Pray, asking God which kind of ministry He is calling you to fulfill. Decide which innovative writing assignment you might accept from God. If He calls you to write about a new issue, take heart. He'll equip you to handle the issues and help people unable to help themselves.

You will find all kinds of resources online with lists of ministries in the areas of church staff–led ministries, denomination-led ministries, lay-led ministries, evangelistic ministry, women's/men's ministries, ministries to the poor (food ministries, clothes closets), the sick (chaplaincy, 12-step programs, support groups, nursing home ministries), the elderly (words of inspiration, retirement living), affinity groups (including sports teams, small groups in churches, agricultural/gardening ministries, and others).

Go to polarisproject.org for information on human-trafficking ministries; salvationarmyusa.org for information on clothing and shelter ministries; namb.net for state missions information; imb.org for information about missions around the world. MyMISSIONfulfilled.com is a site for young women wanting to become involved in missions and offers suggestions on how to do that.

COMPANIONSHIP

Jill shyly slipped into a round-robin group share-time of writers in ministry. As she sat in a chair on the back row, the leader asked everyone to divide into circles according to the kind of ministries for which they had a passion. Jill jumped into the first circle she came to, not knowing the labels for the round-robin groups, and hoping no one would notice her. The woman beside her stood and said, "Please help me. I want to write for women's shelters. I was once out of work and on the streets, and I stayed in a Christian shelter for a long time. I just finished college with a degree in journalism, but I want to use my Christian passion to write materials for shelters. God has called me to give back the comfort they gave me 15 years ago."

I can't believe it, thought Jill. *That's exactly what I want to do when I finish school.* After the session, she talked to Madison, the other writer. Jill shared that she, too, had been out of work and in a shelter that needed many things to help the ministry improve. It had few written materials about the services, no attractive slick pamphlets to enlist funds at fund-raisers, and no Bible studies or devotions to encourage those who lacked everything in life.

If you're looking for companionship and friendships from other Christian writers, try writing in ministries where you both share the same passion. Jill later said, "I had no friends a year ago, but that round-robin group changed my life. I found a more well-balanced life with realistic goals. I knew no one would understand that I wanted to write for the poorest of the poor, for people who had nothing and were afraid for their lives as they slept on the streets. Writing for such a ministry might seem like a pitiful 5-year plan to success, but God had called me to write and to give to this shelter. I was not motivated by earning a large salary or having success in the eyes of the world, as some graduates are. I wanted to obey the call from God, help hurting women, and give them Jesus! Today I'm able give a small bandage to a woman with a scraped knee, a cup of juice for a diabetic with shaky hands, or a blanket to a shivering woman coming in out of the cold. And here's the best part: I can tell them what Jesus means to me!"

Madison agreed. "Today I write grants for several women's shelter ministries. Jill taught me how to do it, since she had experience in that area. I taught her other ministry skills I knew. We're writing a book together about our missions adventures. We and another girl call ourselves the Three Musketeers because we have found a closeness like sisters."

"We're sisters in Christ," said Jill, "and that's a fact."

Think of other creative ways your Creator may be nudging you to minister to His children and find Christian friends along the way.

THE MISSIONARY IN YOU

1. Do you have a vision of your ministry as one for a local church, a homeless women's shelter, a food pantry, or a soup kitchen? Explain.

2. Do you see your ministry as one in a denominational office in your state? How about as a missionary in another part of the world? Explain.

3. Which other cultures could you minister to? Do you have a passion for a group with another language or ethnicity? How

could God be leading you to become a better writer to help communicate to someone who doesn't understand your culture?

4. As a ministering writer, what would you be willing to sacrifice to tell others about Jesus?

THE WRITER IN YOU

1. Why do you think Christian writers have a special companionship or fellowship that is rewarding?

2. Why do you think Jill was not motivated by a successful writing job with a large salary?

3. Make a list of possible writing genres you can see as a ministry to a hurting world.

4. It takes a really good writer to explain some of the churchy words listed in this chapter to those who have never heard of Jesus. Suppose God called you to do this. How would you begin?

A WRITER'S PRAYER

O God, forgive me when I whine and seek You with complaints. Give me an outward heart, concerned for those who have physical, emotional, social, psychological, and other needs in this world. May I write the words You have given me and write only in Your Spirit and Your will. Bless others through my written and spoken words. Because You are the Creator, help me to see the creative in others as I minister to their needs in Jesus' name, amen.

Leadership: The Final Stage of Writing for Christ

WRITING FOR MULTIPLICATION—
THE DUPLICATING STAGE OF
WRITING FOR CHRIST

But you will receive power when the Holy Spirit comes on you; and you will be my witnesses in Jerusalem, and in all Judea and Samaria, and to the ends of the earth.

ACTS 1:8

Miss Jamie led a motley crew of five- and six-year-olds to make a sandbox with paper-doll Bedouin Arabs, wooden camels, and handkerchief tents! Bible stories came alive with the likes of Abraham, Isaac, and Jacob wandering through desert dunes! That summer Jim Martin and his sister, Mary, went home and made their own handmade Hebrew children, playing in their backyard sand.

When she was 12, Miss Jamie appeared again as the leader of preteen girls. To be honest, she wasn't an outstanding leader, but she served faithfully every Thursday afternoon, nudging Mary and other girls to lead programs about missions in faraway lands. She taught them how to write and act in short plays about missionaries. What memories they have today!

Twelve years later Miss Jamie had become Jamie. Mary was an adult with two small children and Jamie was again her leader—this time of young adult women—as she gave them a vision of the world wider than they could imagine. She taught the young women about changing the status quo. They wrote letters to editors and senators, urging change. She taught them about the power of the written word and how to use words responsibly. Sometimes she read minutes from a women's organization that had begun 100 years before. She inspired the younger women from these words about courageous women in their past. Jamie cultivated a passion in Mary and her friends, training Christian leaders to have compassion like Jamie's generation and her grandmother's generation.

"Our chief want is someone who will inspire us to be what we know we could be."

—RALPH WALDO EMERSON

If you have the heart of a Christian writer, your growing maturity will naturally usher you into leadership roles.

WRITER LEADER ON MISSION

Purpose-led believers want to be *on mission* for Christ, with an evangelistic purpose in everything we do. We recognize the gift of writing God gives us and the power He pours into our words. Even Job, struggling with difficult circumstances in life, was aware of the Spirit-filled words inside his heart: "For I am full of words, and the Spirit compels me" (Job 32:18). When tragedies hit—sometimes in the busiest hours of our lives and sometimes in quiet moments—*something compels us* to share our words. And that *something* is Someone—the true Holy Spirit of the Living God.

Part of changing the world is sharing God's love with future as well as present leaders. God calls us to use our writing skills to pour our hearts into articles and books for future generations of believers to read. God also brings younger people into our lives, often nudging us to mentor others as writers on mission. God may have led you to younger—or spiritually younger—writers. Or you may find examples in the Scriptures, such as Paul and Timothy, Elizabeth and Mary, or Naomi and Ruth. Mother-in-law Naomi poured her heart and soul into her young *merea* ([mah-RAY-ah]; Hebrew, feminine form, "dear young friend"). Naomi left Moab (today's Baghdad) and on the long walk home taught her daughter-in-law Ruth Jewish traditions before they arrived in Bethlehem, Naomi's hometown. She probably warned Ruth not to bring a ham to the Jewish family reunion! Naomi became protector, provider, and adviser for Ruth, eventually arranging for Ruth to marry their kinsman redeemer, Boaz. Ruth, a Gentile from Moab, became the great-grandmother of King David.

Like Naomi, our experience has given us words to speak or write as a legacy for future generations. As you have read this book, you may have focused on your passion in life. Are you, like godly Naomi, desiring to leave a legacy of words and/or writing instructions to a younger merea? If so, you can respond to God's call to mentor other speakers and writers. What are some directions you might seek to duplicate yourself as Mary and Jim's leader-mentor Jamie and the Bible character Naomi did?

D DOWN

Most of us start any task by looking down. Sometimes God asks us to bow before Him, on our knees in obedience. Have you ever noticed writers who are too egotistical to look down?

Several years ago, a famous writer and his wife checked into a hotel where he was to speak the next day. A pastor stood behind him in line. When the writer asked for his reserved room, the desk clerk replied he didn't have his name listed, but he'd secure another one.

"What?" the writer said. "What do you *mean*, you don't have my name listed?" He turned red.

"Sir," said the clerk, "I'll be glad to give you our best suite. Just spell your name."

The writer pounded on the registration desk and shouted a few choice words.

The wife looked at the pastor behind them, who instantly looked down at the floor.

"Please, Honey, be quiet," she whispered. "People are staring!"

The writer ignored her. "I will *not* be quiet! I want to speak to the manager. Now!"

The manager arrived shortly, assuring the writer he'd receive a nice room. With a haughty stamp, the writer snatched the keys to a penthouse room. "It's about time!" he said, avoiding his wife's harsh look. He grabbed her arm, took a giant step—and promptly stumbled over his suitcase, falling flat on his face.

Everyone nearby laughed, including his wife, the clerk, the manager, and the pastor.

Our lofty goals are wonderful, but writing *on mission* requires down-to-earth hard work and obedience. We are compelled to pause and look down to see what's at our feet. A good leader never stops learning. He or she is diligent with basics before moving beyond them. As writers master grammar, style, point of view, and other nuts and bolts of writing, we share them with others. If our editors suggest a few pointers about habitual errors, then we seek advice from other writers and professional experts in the field on how to improve our craft.

Some Christian writers make the mistake of thinking their calls or their gifts are better than those of others. Writers can fall into the trap of *gift despisement*, condescending as they look at other writers' gifts. We are prideful, unwilling to let anyone critique our writing because we think every precious word we keyed in is a gift from God. Some writers feel their *book* is a better genre than another writer's *newsletter*; or they believe their *first-page news article* is better than the passionate *column* in the Religion section. Who knows how God can use all our efforts in His evangelism of the world through His Holy Spirit's movement in the hearts of men and women? To bring our writing under the control of Christ means we humbly give everything we write to Him as a sacrifice of praise. Hebrews 13:15–17 says,

> *Let us continually offer to God a sacrifice of praise—the fruit of lips that confess his name. And do not forget to do good and to share with others, for with such sacrifices God is pleased. Obey your leaders and submit to their authority. They keep watch over you as men who must give an account. [The work of leadership is] a joy, not a burden.*

Being willing to accept correction or constructive criticism is often called *Christlike humility*. Leadership in writing calls for a give-and-take spirit. We clean up the area around our feet: maintaining excellence in Christian work, as a writer someone would want to follow.

 U P

Becoming a writing leader reflects an upward spirit. Ask God to guide your hands as you show other writers how to key in words in a worshipful attitude. Pray you can show them how to find concepts that only He can provide. Christian writers deliberately stay away from shallow water and avoid splashing around in the murky, banal ideas of others. They explore new topics or themes, deciding on devices and methods to convey them. Then they share the writing craft with others.

What might God be calling you to do, above your wildest dreams? Don't think small; think *outside yourself* but *inside God's power* to perform miracles, with your desire to share your call to writing. What is *His* vision, *His* mission through you? How can He use your feet and hands to accomplish His purpose? How can He use your writing talent to change the world for future generations?

As you have gained practical experience in the world—sometimes on the firing line—define solutions you've discovered and educate younger Christian writers. Ask for confidence to share. Pray young writers will take up the Christian banner, stepping over barriers in publication and communications.

A AROUND

What is close to you now—maybe in the palm of your hand? Look around for opportunities to lead in writing arenas. As sacred obedience to the Father, begin at home. Like Naomi, you may have family members who need your expertise. Does Uncle Johnny dream of writing missionary memoirs? Does Cousin Nancy need help with family genealogies? Think of ways to mentor those closest to you who are thinking of writing.

Any futurist can tell you one of the greatest needs for this century is mentoring. Observe the needs for writers in your community, your work areas, or your networking circles who need encouragement or training. Look around you and listen to God.

I INWARD

At least three kinds of characteristics lie deep within you. Look inward at your leadership ability through your God-given natural talents, learned skills, and spiritual gifts. Which of your traits can fulfill needs of other Christian writers?

Natural talents. Do you have the innate flair for a smooth writing style? Do beautiful words flow out of your head onto the lighted screen or white paper before you, almost at will? Some of your friends or teachers may have said you were a born writer or you have natural talent. You may have inherited a natural propensity for good persuasive prose, like your father, mother, or extended family. Consider how His Spirit could use your God-given talents to make the world a better place and change people's confusion to peace and faith.

Learned skills. Just as you learned how to play the piano or the trumpet, you have learned other skills as a writer. Editing homework papers in your early grades, working on a school newspaper, or helping poor children learn to read may be hidden skills you've never thought of using for evangelization. Through experience in Bible study, you may have the learned skill of comparing passages of Scripture to the situations in life. You may have learned a special knack of interpretation of difficult passages or of language translation from Greek and Hebrew. Search your past for any skills you have that God can use for *His mission.*

Spiritual gifts. Every Christian possesses a unique combination of traits to share God's love with others. The spiritual gift of administration could be useful in helping other writers organize their book proposals. If you have the gift of mercy, you'll have a passion for helping struggling scribblers solve their writing problems. If you have the gift of teaching, you'll find ways to teach them how to communicate clearly. You may be a natural encourager who could eliminate a negative attitude in a potential Christian writer or show an uneducated writer how to write her Christian autobiography of faith for 50 unchurched family members! What is inside your body, soul, or spirit that another author or a potential writer could use for God's glory?

B BACK

Writers often approach the past to improve the future. Recall timeless principles in your own experiences to help another writer. Begin by listing (1) lessons you've learned from the hard knocks of life and (2) ways to share practical suggestions for transforming life into fiction or nonfiction. From our own life situations, each of us can write practical instructions in spiritual formation,

Christian growth, and godly perspectives on maturity—or perhaps instructions on the framework of a good fiction story.

Some writers have metal baskets labeled "Fodder." When an experience or idea happens, they jot it down and toss it into the fodder file for future use. If you have an idea like that one, show another writer your method. How do you acquire subject ideas? Ideas can come from everywhere: a childhood incident, your family's past joys and tragedies, a book you read as a teen, or a YouTube video that jogs your memory to an event in your past.

As we wrote earlier in this book, God is economical, never wasting any experience He allowed to touch your life. Whether a horrible nightmare or a bountiful blessing, every piece of the jigsaw puzzle we call *life* fits perfectly, succinctly into His pattern. A missions trip to a dangerous country, for instance, can become a lesson in trusting God—so the next person's journey there won't be precarious. Leading someone to Christ in an unexpected way may become the introductory story in a chapter of a book on miracles. An incident in child rearing may be fodder for a writer to encourage scared new parents. The prophet Isaiah has recorded these words from God: "'You are my witnesses,' declares the Lord, 'and my servant whom I have chosen'" (Isaiah 43:10).

Vonda Skelton, a South Carolina writer, tells of a time in a dark house with no lights, looking through a pile of papers to help a relative in crisis. Stumbling in the dark, God spoke to her: *This would make a good Christian fiction novel!* She laughed aloud, realizing God uses everything in our lives—every weird detail—to prepare us for Christian writing. Each of us has a set of unique parameters from which we pull ideas and "holy suggestions." Look back and see how God can combine your past and your passion for leadership today.

In 1886, Sarah Clarke, codirector of Chicago's Pacific Garden Mission, led a baseball player, William "Billy" Ashley Sunday, to accept Jesus into his heart. After helping at the mission with "Ma

Clarke," Billy later turned down $400 a month playing for the Chicago White Stockings team (average American salary: *$480 per year*) to become an evangelist. From the 1880s till the 1930s Billy Sunday led sawdust-and-tent revivals all over America, preaching to more than 100 million people—without loudspeakers, TV, or radio.

One night a young man came forward to accept Jesus as Savior, and like Billy Sunday, Mordecai Fowler Ham became an evangelist. In 1934, a year before Billy Sunday died, Ham led revivals in Charlotte, North Carolina, where he stirred up controversy. A door-to-door Fuller Brush salesman who came to hear about the controversy was convicted of his own sin and committed his life to Christ. His name was Billy Graham.

From Sarah Clarke to Billy Graham, a legacy of evangelism and spiritual disciples evolved. Where would we be today without this link of the Holy Spirit from one heart to another? What a legacy Ma Clarke began!

> How about you? You may not be called to be an evangelist, but your words are just as important to the Lord as those of Billy Sunday or Billy Graham.

How do you pass along your legacy as a writing leader? Through the quiet words of a mother like Sarah Clarke, the exuberant gyrations of a prohibitionist like Billy Sunday, the stern condemnation of a preacher like Mordecai Ham, or the straightforward sermons of a crusader like Billy Graham? Today the same Holy Spirit still chooses each Christian's uniqueness as His method of spreading His Word to the next generation.

Our own personalities often determine the leadership role we take. You can't lead out of gifts or traits you don't have. Each of us passes along our legacy in our own way.

Be yourself. As God leads, you discover your leadership ministry as *uniquely you.* Because of who God is, your leadership in a writing ministry will come out of *who you are in Him* and *what you know about Him.* Think how God may take your passion and allow you to lead others to be writers on mission for Him. God may have chosen you *for such a time as this* (Esther 4:14).

CHOOSING A DIRECTION FOR
YOUR LEADERSHIP MINISTRY

After looking down, up, around, inward, and back, while searching the Holy Sprit's influence on *your spirit,* look for practical ways to use your talents, skills, and gifts to lead *others on mission* for God. You can use the following mentoring roles as ways to lead others to join Him in His mission for redeeming the world.

TEACHING

Why not ask other writers to join you monthly for a critique group to encourage each other? Set a time and place, share samples of your work, and allow time for everyone's opinion on things like style, easy flow, clarity, compelling plot, and/or a focused point of view. Give strengths and weaknesses of each work. If you feel led, offer a nuts-and-bolts teaching workshop for beginning writers. You don't have to know everything about the English language or marketing strategies; just show the critique group what you've learned that works for you. Share ideas or handouts from writers conferences you've attended or refer writers to helpful Web sites.

COUNSELING

From the nugget of an idea for a magazine article to the final royalties of a sizable book, writers need wise counsel. As God leads, help budding authors find God's will for their writing. Pray about writing careers. Celebrate published works and comfort one another after rejection letters. Encourage group counseling, as one young writer can, in turn, become an adviser to a beginner. The prophet Malachi says, "Those who feared the Lord consulted with each other and... a book of remembrance was written in his presence" (Malachi 3:16).

 MODELING

Because of your experience, you can become a model for younger writers. Try the "dog-and-flea" leadership method: ask a fledgling writer to follow your lead as you attend regional Christian conferences, writers retreats, or creative writing classes. (Think of it as a merea hopping on the shoulder of the mentor and getting a free ride, like a flea on a dog's back.) Pay a young writer's way to a training event, or give him or her scholarships when possible. Show a novice writer your writing files as a model of good organization, or model a good attitude of unselfishness as you share your ideas for success. Whether we want to or not, each writer is a role model for other writers, positive or negative.

ENCOURAGING

One of the best ways we can help writers is simply to encourage them. Have you ever had one of those days when someone's smile would have made your day—but no one smiled? Christian writers love to give smiles freely, hug as needed, and write notes on special occasions. Compliment writers on their unselfish service. Host a party to celebrate an accepted manuscript or send an email blitz to lead inexperienced

POSSIBLE CHRISTIAN LEADERSHIP POSITIONS FOR WRITERS:

- Mentoring other writers or speakers
- Editing for newsletters and magazines
- Designing lifestyle coaching materials
- Writing instructions for others to begin a ministry
- Leading a small critique group for writers
- Helping others leave a legacy for future generations in their churches or families

writers into networking with others. Some writers have learned to take time to look up books by fellow writers and write a positive review on a social network such as Facebook or Twitter. Encourage writer wannabes to encourage others who already have works published. Show them what you've learned about investing your life in the lives of other writers. (For these and other ways to mentor others, read *Woman to Woman: Preparing Yourself to Mentor* [NewHopeDigital.com] or *Seeking Wisdom: Preparing Yourself to Be Mentored* [EdnaEllison.com].)

Don't underestimate the power of your words. Face-to-face, shower other writers with encouraging words, which go all the way to the bone. "Pleasant words are a honeycomb, sweet to the soul and healing to the bones" (Proverbs 16:24).

Above all, leave a legacy of leadership as you share with inexperienced authors about the call of a Christian writer. God's call lies far above any other secular impulse to write. God may call us to be leaders of one or of millions. Writing on mission is all about Him, not us. Be open and creative as the Creator leads. Think of your leadership as a blank slate on which God will reveal opportunities in His Light. We are limited only by our lack of creativity and hope. Without hesitation, remember these words in Isaiah: "This is what the Lord says, he who created you . . . 'I have summoned you by name; you are mine. . . . Since you are precious and honored in my sight, and because I love you. . . . Do not be afraid, for I am with you'" (Isaiah 43:1, 4–5).

THE MISSIONARY IN YOU

1. How do you believe your *passion* for writing has changed? How has it grown?

2. What do think it means to look down and "clean up around your feet"?

3. What may God be calling you to do in world evangelization *beyond your wildest dreams?*

4. What do you think may be huge barriers to the gospel in the world today? How could you help break down some of the barriers through your writing ministry?

THE WRITER IN YOU

1. How might you fulfill God's call to become a writer/mentor?

2. Of teaching, counseling, modeling, and encouraging others, which of the mentoring roles in this chapter is your favorite? Why?

3. What kinds of stories, newspaper items, or favorite quotations can you think of now to toss into your fodder file for future consumption in your writing?

4. As you pray, how can you submit to *His leadership* in your writing?

A WRITER'S PRAYER

Lord, help me become an effective writer on mission with Your vision. Help me accept criticism and correction as I hone the skills You've given me. Give me Christlike humility in all I do. Bless my words and allow them to lead others. Thank You for opportunities to mentor others as I have been mentored by other Christian writers. Because You gave Your life for me, may I share my life with other writers as a servant leader for You. In Jesus' name, amen.

The Basics of Writing for Christian Leadership

FOR DUPLICATING LEADERS—HOW TO WRITE UNDER CHRIST'S LEADERSHIP

Now to him who is able to do immeasurably more than all we ask or imagine, according to his power that is at work within us, to him be glory in the church and in Christ Jesus throughout all generations, forever and ever! Amen.

EPHESIANS 3:20–21

When Joy heard her pastor say, "More slaves live in the world today than in 1880," she was alarmed. *Surely her pastor must have been wrong! How could it be? Slavery was a thing of the past. Surely the world had grown more civilized in the last two centuries!* After tucking her children in bed that night and praying with them as usual, Joy could not get comfortable in her bed, unable to sleep. Though Bill slept quietly beside her, she felt alone. The burden of people being exploited across her own nation and even more helpless victims in other nations weighed heavily on her heart. She was only one woman, and not a very strong leader at that. How could God expect her to do anything about evil all over the world? Why had she even listened to the truth at church that Sunday? She tossed and turned all night long, and the next morning, after saying good-bye to her husband and taking the children to school, she left the breakfast cereal dishes in the sink and began to search online for facts about human trafficking and other human exploitation tragedies worldwide. An hour later, she was blown away by what she had discovered. It was true: 27 million people were slaves in the postmodern world! Millions of them existed in her own country.

All that week, Joy prayed for God to show her how to lead her missions groups to do something about the situation. She discussed it with Bill, and he was also concerned.

"For the sake of our children," he said, "we've got to do something about this in our generation. We can't let Jack, Turner, and Elizabeth grow up in a world like that." He suggested they watch a reality television program that night about slavery. To their surprise, one of the scenes took place in their own state! Bill called their local sheriff and asked him to speak in their home a few days later. Several more couples in their Bible study group joined them to find out the truth. After listening to the law enforcement report, Joy was sick at heart. Women, teens, and even some men and very young children had been transported through their town on an interstate highway to supply prostitutes and other exploited people for sale at the Super Bowl celebrations that year. As they listened, Joy felt overwhelmed. Her spirit wanted to do something, but she didn't feel God was calling her to attack the problem.

As Joy sat in her living room, stunned at what she had heard, her friend Martha stood up. "I feel called to do something about this," she said. "As you know, my children have just married and left the state for good jobs elsewhere, and I'm not working outside the home now. I have more free time than I've ever had. It's as if God has just cleared my calendar to do this for Him. I don't know how to get started, but I am praying God will show us how. How many of you will help me, if I can lead this group?" One couple had to leave early, but the others stayed late, planning to organize a task force, with liaisons to law enforcement, safe houses, social services facilities, church ministries, and other services in the community that would be needed for a united front against such evil. They ended the evening with prayer. One man finished his prayer with, "Lord, have mercy on our souls."

After everyone left that night, Joy sat down at her computer and began typing. "I want to lead an awareness campaign," she said to Bill. "Most people right here in town don't even know about this evil practice."

"Sure they do, honey," he said. "At least some of them know. They just choose to ignore it." Let's get a flyer with facts finished tonight so they can't ignore it anymore." Within a few days, they had generated interest with the flyer distributed all over town. People met at their church to see who could help and which kinds of volunteers were needed. Some people backed off from the ministry, feeling it was too sordid to get involved in, but many wanted to help.

Joy became a leader in the awareness campaign, while Bill and others helped, each in his or her own way, according to their passions, talents, skills, and gifts. College students at a nearby school organized a walkathon to raise funds, and the community joined to make a difference in their world. A year later, the women of Joy's church had organized mentoring groups for young women coming from abuse situations. Local agencies banded together to help provide counseling for those who came out of prostitution, and hundreds of volunteers raised funds for housing and other needs for exploited people. Their state legislature passed two strong laws after groups, including Martha's, demonstrated for days on the state house steps. Joy designed posters and pamphlets to distribute, and Martha organized 25 women who wrote letters and stamped envelopes to send to their representatives in their state capital. Local law enforcement enforced these laws and many criminals were arrested for human exploitation.

"How does this sound?" Joy said one day to Bill, reading from a booklet she had written.

> A year ago, organized crime in our area had changed from selling drugs to selling people. It was more profitable here to sell humans. They could sell drugs only once. Humans could be sold many times in one night to different people every half hour. Here we are, one year later, with human exploitation much lower. You have made a difference! Join us for the next step. Every household can claim their block for zero crime or any kind of abuse or human trafficking. Let's stamp out exploitation in our lifetimes with a zero tolerance!

"You go, girl" Bill said. "You are getting the word out! We're going to do this in our generation!"

Several years later, Joy was writing a manual on how to organize Christian volunteers to clean up communities and stop the worst of crimes. She was also teaching other writers how to write curriculum for girls' homes to help young girls get an education as they recovered from abuse. The need is great for Christian social services instructions, for awareness pamphlets in every location, for Bible studies for Christian counselors to use, and for witnessing leaflets to assure abuse victims they are chosen by God to be "holy and blameless in his sight" (Ephesians 1:4). You can be a part of something big as you join God as a writer on mission to address this issue. And here's the best part: this is only one issue. God has many areas where He can use your talent and your willingness to serve Him!

HOW TO BE A LEADER AS A WRITER ON MISSION

Joy was just one woman who used her writing skills to serve God in His mission of love for all abused, unchurched people. He has given you talents, skills, and gifts to serve Him as a writer and a leader who can influence others. What are your tentative plans to use your personality, time, funds, and energy also as a missions-hearted writer in a leadership role?

Law of Exponential Re-creation

How many leaders can one writer duplicate if he or she multiplies himself or herself four times?

1

2 2

4 4 4 4

16 16 16 16 16 16 16 16

256 256 256 256 256 256 256 256 256 256 256 256 256 256 256 256

LAW OF EXPONENTIAL RE-CREATION

As you show others what you have found is useful in writing for the kingdom of God, you can train younger writers. As you do, you'll find the need for training trainers. They in turn will go out and train others. Use the laws of exponential re-creation: multiply yourself exponentially through your advice to younger women in your church, your own children, and/or neighborhood children (in local organizations or parachurch groups) as well as your church family. Make your grandchildren your *mereas* (mentees or protégés). Befriend others who learn how to write from you in church classes or informal teaching institutes in your local area.

Start small. Major on the minors; pay attention to details. Take one or two young people at a time and pass along your legacy of writing. Help them take ownership of one writing project at a time. Become life coaches to teach them how to live, submitting to the Lord, as you teach them to write on mission. Invest in their lives and you will observe the law of exponential re-creation (not to be confused with *recreation*, but it's fine to have a little fun and enjoy sports as you build relationships with young writers on mission!) As Creator, God will show you how to be creative as you re-create leaders, model leadership, and teach them to lead others. He is the Master of miracles. Let the leadership flow naturally, and let small starts explode exponentially: 1 grows to 2; 2 grows to 4; 4 grows to 16, 16 grows to 256, etc. Dream big. It's a God-sized dream.

MANUALS

How does a training manual differ from other kinds of writing? Remember, as you write nonfiction Christian training manuals, they usually contain a rationale, a biblical basis for all you do, a scope and sequence of the projects, as described in chapter 12, and detailed procedures for the work. A manual will be organized logically with coherence building from stage to stage. It will need one or two overarching objectives, composed of smaller step-by-step goals, with each goal composed of smaller aims. It will contain directional passages with procedures:

Wrong: Have the students write a bunch of values.
Right: Ask each student to write a list of eight Christian values for a pamphlet to be distributed on May 20.

Procedures, like goals, should be SMART: specific, measurable, attainable, realistic, and timely. Specific procedures set a clear aim and offer step-by-step stages of success to reach it. Measurable procedures usually have numbers or other items that can be measured to see whether or not you've succeeded. They might use words like *count, list, memorize-and-recite,* or *show*. Attainable procedures are not far-reaching. They begin with one simple step that's easy to reach and then progress to other steps which build on the first one to get to a higher level. **Realistic** procedures do not use words like *dream, hope, imagine,* or *pretend.* Get in the real world! Think of negatives with your writing project as well as positives so you can approach them realistically. Timely procedures block off small increments of your day for writing in a certain way. For instance, if you know you have to help your spouse wash three loads of clothes and pay all the monthly bills on the first day of next week, don't plan an eight-hour writing marathon on that day.

Examples:
Specific: Research and list the Christian values I plan to write in chapter 3.

Measurable: Research and list the four Christian values I plan to write in chapter 3.

Realistic: Research and list two of the four Christian values I plan to write in chapter 3.

Attainable: Rearrange carpool commitment on Thursday; research and list two Christian values I plan to write in chapter 3.

Timely: List two Christian values I plan to write in chapter 3 before 2:30 P.M. on Thursday, January 15.

Smart: Thursday, January 15, before 2:30: Rearrange my carpool commitment; research and list two of the four Christian values I plan to write in chapter 3.

Do a SMART check in each of these five areas for each procedure you write. Surround your planning, implementing, and follow-up evaluation goals with prayer.

Susan High, director of Wellspring Living, a project for abused women in a midsized city, was eager to move forward with her ministry's project of obtaining land, building a dorm, and housing abused women. Then she picked up the book *Circle Maker*, by Mark Batterson.

Susan said, "The story of the Circle Maker happened between the Old Testament and the New Testament. The village people had waited hundreds of years without hearing Gods' voice. Then they prayed fervently in their circle, holding up their prayers and dreams to Him—and soon God gave them Jesus!

"My 40 days of prayer have been the biggest encouragement to my prayer life. At first, I hesitated to take this time, feeling I had goals to accomplish, but I heard God's Spirit say, 'Susan, do you remember what kind of panties you have?' I was shocked, but thought of my good underwear, the not-so-good, the larger and more comfortable, the small and tighter, the flimsy, the strong—every woman knows what I mean. I know this sounds ridiculous, but God said, 'Get out your big girl panties, Susan—your praying panties—and start earnest prayer.' I began that day, and since then I have felt a fresh wind blowing through my ministry. I have found sweet encouragement, no matter how far behind I have been on *my* goals."

Susan also shared her ministry's mission statement:

Wellspring Living: Connects a caring community with women seeking a way out of unhealthy lifestyles, promoting healing, wholeness, independence, and family restoration through biblical principles.

Above all else, guard your heart, for it is the wellspring of life.

PROVERBS 4:23

God sometimes takes us away from our own goals and sets us aside
for a spiritual refreshment. He knows we need our physical shells
peeled away. He knows we also need to peel away the hard shells of
our souls—the centers of our will, our emotions, and our intellect—
so that His Holy Spirit can mingle with ours. What sweet peace
and joy fills our deep-core spirits when we set aside everything else
to fellowship with Him!

Make sure your leadership goals are God's, not yours. Also, if
you're a Christian writer, God called you to be a *writer on mission*.
He didn't call you to be a *publisher on mission*. Once you've sent off
your work to a publisher, let it go. Sometimes our own minds want
to take over. We want to direct the world! When you release your
work to a publisher, don't call with petty questions; don't criticize
the editor; don't redesign the cover. With the gentle spirit of hope,
allow professionals to handle your work.

 CHARACTERISTICS

Good writer-leaders encourage others and are always positive and
optimistic around those that help them. You can help morale by
being fair and kind, as you offer rewards for good work. Whether
you have a staff or just volunteers or family to help you, be good
communicators not only in your written words but also in your
spoken words to those who help you most. Pray with them often.
Take time to care about their lives. They will take ownership of
your ideas, projects, and plans if you empower them by giving
God's encouragement to them. Great Christian writers are well
organized, communicating a clear desire to serve God and get the
job done!

INVOLVEMENT

Involve as many people as you can in your writing adventures. Ask
prayer triplets (groups of three) to pray for you and with you. Let

others help as you lead; don't do everything yourself. Encourage readers to be writers and writers to be readers. (See chap. 6 for ideas on a platform from which you can help your publisher in promotion and marketing.) Empower your readers and learners to fulfill their usefulness to the Lord according to their personalities. What kinds of promotion or marketing could volunteers do for you? Many writers have others to tweet for them, go through their email, or participate in Facebook with their fans.

Above all, pray for your leadership in your writing as God leads you and your audience to focus on His mission for the world.

After Paul communicates messages to a long list of fellow workers, volunteers in the church in Colossae, he says, "And pray for us, too, that God may open a door for our message, so that we may proclaim the mystery of Christ. Pray that I may proclaim it clearly as I should" (Colossians 4:3–4). At the end of his list, he also sends one last message to a church worker named Archippus: "See to it that you complete the work you have received in the Lord." As writers we need to see to it we finish the task of writing. Don't just dream about writing and never complete your assignment. Use your iron will and your tender spirit to sit down in your writing chair and finish what you start. (You might be surprised at how many good writers procrastinate and never finish any assignment God gives them to write!) He says, "Be strong and do the work! (1 Chronicles 28:10).

LEADERSHIP: THE FINAL STAGE OF WRITING FOR CHRIST

We chose the above words as the chapter title for the last chapter for writers. Although leadership and self-duplication is the assumed highest step on a writer's ladder to success, can there ever be a *final stage of writing* for Christ? No matter what our efforts, we will never reach that final stage. As long as we live, He'll have His call on our lives. At some point in our older years, we may *re-tire*, but that simply means we put new tires on our cars and keep on going. Our prayer is that God will give you a vision for your present and future leadership, and that you will be faithful to fulfill it.

God says, "Write the vision. . . . Wait for it; because it will surely come"
(HABAKKUK 2:2–3)

THE MISSIONARY IN YOU

1. If you feel a call from God to be a missionary, how can you use your leadership skills on a missions field?
2. What kinds of written materials might a local or overseas missionary leader need?
3. If you feel God has called you to be a missionary writer from your home, what leadership projects has He called to your mind?
4. How can you be obedient to a home-based writing ministry in your local area?
5. Using the law of exponential re-creation, how many people do you think you can reach through your writing in the next two years? Remember, those who don't set a goal seldom reach it.

THE WRITER IN YOU

1. As you pray, do you feel God is calling you to be a Christian writer? How can you submit to *His* leadership in *your* writing?
2. On a scale of 1 to 10, where do you think you stand as a Christian leader? How can you grow?
3. Look at the quote from Habakkuk 2 above. What sort of vision do you have for your leadership in multiplying others to become a writer on mission?
4. Check your calendar now and reserve some writing time for beginning a future writing project. May God bless you as you avoid procrastination!

A WRITER'S PRAYER

O God, as I finish this book, help me remember Your important precepts. May I not just dream about writing, but get busy and write for You. Let me write to inspire my family, my community, and my world. Thank You for a spiritual relationship with You, Scripture as a basis, a Christian worldview, my relationships with others, the ability to communicate Christ to them, my personal ministry to people in need, and my leadership among other Christians. In Jesus' name, amen.

Conclusion

This book contains only a small amount of what writers need to know about writing. The intent was never to teach writing but to help writers to recognize and solidify *the call* of writing.

Once a person has heard God speak clearly to him or her about becoming a writer, there is usually a period of apprehension—a time when many thoughts inhibit yielding completely to the call. Some of those thoughts may include:

"Who, me?"
Yes, you. If God clearly says to you, "I need you to write and tell the world about Me," you have no other choice if you are a Christian man or woman who wants to be obedient to God. Christians often quote this saying in situations such as this—"God doesn't call the equipped; He equips the called." If you hear God saying "write" to you, do everything you can to become the best writer you can be. Study, learn, interact with other writers, pray, and write.

"I don't know how to write. I flunked English twice."
A writer on mission doesn't get graded on his or her writing performance. You can learn through books such as this how to write well and communicate your message with clarity. And, if you still struggle with a command of the language, you can get your message down on paper or into a computer file, and then hire an editor to check grammar, punctuation, and word usage. When writing for publication to reach the world for Jesus, the only grade you need to worry about is getting an A in obedience to God.

"There are thousands, maybe millions, of writers already. Why would I even have a chance of being successful?"

Millions of other authors may be writing, but there is only one you! You are the only one who can write the message God has given you. You are the only one who has your unique perspective on life. The messages may be similar but the things you write and the things other writers write will be uniquely from the writer's perspective.

Think about the four Gospels. Four men walked closely with Jesus and experienced many of the same events. Were their accounts identical? No! God called four different writers of different backgrounds and personalities to give us a more complete picture of Jesus Christ and to reach readers who could identify more closely with each writer.

Matthew's audience was Hebrew and he wrote to show that the long-awaited Messiah had come, citing Old Testament evidence that proved the claims believers were making about Jesus. Matthew's emphasis is on Jesus as the promised King. "This took place to fulfill what was spoken through the prophet: 'Say to the Daughter of Zion, "See, your king comes to you, gentle and riding on a donkey, on a colt, the foal of a donkey"'" (Matthew 21:4–5).

Mark's audience was Gentile and his emphasis is on Jesus as the Suffering Servant. Much of this Gospel focuses on the suffering and sacrifice of the last week of Jesus' life. He stated the focus of his book in Mark 10:43–45: "Instead, whoever wants to become great among you must be your servant, and whoever wants to be first must be slave of all. For even the Son of Man did not come to be served, but to serve, and to give his life as a ransom for many."

Luke, a physician who was loved by many people, was a master historian; therefore, he wanted to write an orderly account of the life of Christ. "Therefore, since I myself have carefully investigated everything from the beginning, it seemed good also to me to write an orderly account for you, most excellent Theophilus, so that you may know the certainty of the things you have been taught" (Luke 1:3–4). Writing to his friend Theophilus, Luke had a Gentile audience in mind. He often calls Jesus the Son of man. Many details in Luke's account are left out of other versions.

John included more theological content as to who Jesus was, going back to the beginning to start his account. "In the beginning was the Word, and the Word was with God, and the Word was God. He was with God in the beginning" (John 1:1–2). John emphasizes the deity of Christ but also the fact of His humanity. John had a heart to get the message to the people. "Jesus did many other miraculous signs in the presence of his disciples, which are not recorded in this book. But these are written that you may believe that Jesus is the Christ, the Son of God, and that by believing you may have life in His name" (John 20:30–31).

Four men. Four accounts and perspectives of the same events.

The events you see today and the understanding God gives you of the Scriptures are different from anyone else on the earth. Only you can write it as you see it. Study, pray, and ask God to reveal the unique message He has given you. Then get to your computer and begin writing!

"I think God has called me to write but I don't know how to begin."
If you are reading this book, you have gotten off to a good start. Soak up everything you can about writing by reading good books, attending writers conferences, building a good writing resource library, visiting writing Web sites, and chatting with other writers. Read good books and figure out why the writing is good. Find magazines you would like to write for and examine the format and content of their articles. Yes, it is hard work being a writer. But fulfilling the call of God on your life is not only rewarding and satisfying, it is also *essential* to becoming all God intended you to be.

Don't let negative thoughts flood your mind and discourage you. You know discouragement is not from God. The enemy would like nothing better than for God to call you to a ministry of writing and for you to let insecurities and other things knock you off the path. Don't let that happen.

If God has called you to become a writer on mission, you *are* a writer on mission. Maybe not a fully developed one yet, but deep down inside that writer is waiting to get out. So sit up straight, raise your right hand, and say, "By God's grace and through His direction, I am a writer!" Sometimes that is the hardest first step—to verbalize that you are, indeed, a writer. Don't let that be a stumbling block ever again. You can do it! You are a writer. Go and spread the gospel in print.

William Carey, missionary to India, said, "Expect great things [from God]. Attempt great things [for God]."

A PRAYER FOR THE READER

Dear Father and Lord of our words, bless the reader of this book. Take the time he or she has given to reading Called to Write *and redeem it for Your glory. Give each reader understanding and a desire to apply the principles here. Most of all, inspire each reader to write the message You have given him or her. Grant affirmation of Your calling and fill every heart to overflowing. Help each of us always to make every word count. Amen.*

A Visit with the Authors

1. In today's world, why is it important for a Christian writer to be on mission?

Linda: In today's world, it is important for you to be "on mission" or called by God to whatever you do. A writer is no different. The world is big, and millions of people still don't know about Jesus. Missionaries actually go overseas to tell people personally about Jesus. Face-to-face is a great way to spread the word. Preachers preach in congregations across our nations many times a week and they are doing their best to reach the local people. But what about all the rest? A writer who includes the biblical truth in everything he or she writes and writes from a biblical worldview has the opportunity to reach thousands, if not millions, with a printed message.

So it's important for Christian writers to include the gospel in everything they write whether in specific words, in expressing their worldviews, or in subtle suggestion. God will multiply your efforts, if you are a committed writer on mission.

2. Explain the seven areas of this book.

Edna: Called to Write follows these stages:

1) Spirituality. Through the Holy Spirit, writers can identify whether they possess the overflowing heart with God's Spirit compelling them to write.

2) Scripture study. Once writers possess salvation, inviting Jesus into their hearts and maintaining a personal relationship with Him, they hunger to study the Bible for instructions for Christian writers; they find in His Word a solid foundation for their writing.

3) Worldview. Christian writers filter their writing through a Christian worldview to see the world through the eyes of Christ.

4) Relationships. With a Christ-centered worldview, Christian writers see all their relationships in a new way: they see their influence among others as an opportunity to share Christ.

5) Communication. Once Christian writers recognize their relationships with others, they concentrate on communicating the message of Christ's love clearly to everyone in their sphere of influence.

6) Ministry. Christian writers who communicate with others because of their relationship with Christ will have compassion on hurting people and desire to get involved in ministries to a hurting world.

7) Leadership. Once Christian writers do hands-on ministry, they become leaders in ministering and communicating the message to others. They can duplicate their effectiveness as leaders sharing Christ's love with the world.

It's simple: Spirituality leads to Scripture study, which leads to a Christ-centered worldview, which leads to enhanced relationships, which leads to communication of the gospel, which leads to an outpouring of ministry to a hurting world, which leads to leadership in duplicating this process of a writer on mission.

3. If I know God has called me to be a writer, won't He show me how to do it?

Linda: Of course, the simple answer to that question is yes. But when God calls us to do something, He expects us to do our part. That may mean going back to school, learning about another culture, or for writers, going to a writers conference. God will open doors for you as a Christian writer. But unless you are attentive and observant in the publishing world, you may not recognize those doors.

If you are a Christian writer on mission, work hard to prepare yourself and equip yourself for that mission. God will show you the specific areas where He can best use your talents. As you seek His will through prayer and Bible study, He will direct you and your mission will become clearer.

4. I already have plenty of instructional books on writing. Why is this one different?

Edna: Every Christian writer probably has a stack of books on writing, but they yearn for an instruction book for a writer who is *on mission*, with a well-defined purpose for their writing: sharing the gospel story—that Jesus died for their sins and, as a resurrected Lord, He desires a personal relationship with each of us—with everyone in the world.

This book will help ordinary people who want to write a small spiritual autobiography for their grandchildren as well as a seminary professor who is writing a three-volume work on apologetics. Every Christian in the world, in every strata of life, yearns for a missions-focused instruction book to keep our eyes on Jesus as we write.

5. Will this book help me be a better Christian?

Linda: Our prayer for this book from the beginning is that it would touch writers and encourage them as they discover God's specific plans for their writing. If you are struggling with your faith and feel stagnant in your growth, we would hope the encouragement in this book to study your Bible, pray, seek the counsel of others, and more would give you new direction and bring you closer to the Lord. As you grow as a writer, you will see how God is directing your writing journey; and as you recognize that, you grow closer to Him. As we discussed in the relationship chapter, relationship with God should be the foundation for every Christian writer.

6. I have been writing for a while and already have quite a few articles published. Is there anything new for me to learn?

Edna: Everyone needs a refresher course in writing. *Called to Write* provides a book full of these writing basics, but more than technical skills, this book offers a reminder to let God guide the writing of all Christian authors, to give us courage to use our iron wills to maintain a constant focus on our Christian mission: to write to all people, telling the good news that Jesus offers us the free gift of salvation and a personal relationship with Him. We believe this book offers hope, motivation, and inspiration to stay focused on Christ as we write and influence others for Him.

7. It seems like many publishers today are publishing fewer and fewer books. Is there any hope of a new writer getting published?
Linda: Absolutely! If you are following God's calling to be a writer and have the assurance of His plan for you, you can trust He has a plan for your writing that could very possibly include publication.

Traditional, royalty-paying publishers are publishing fewer books. That doesn't mean they won't publish yours. By all means, create a stellar book proposal and submit it to a publisher as God directs. Publishers are still looking for books of excellence to be part of their catalogs each year. Yours could be one of the ones they are looking for this year!

Today we also have the option of ebooks and self-publishing. Ebooks are becoming very popular and often even if people have a print version of a book, they want an ebook. There are also many ebooks that have never appeared in print format. Many online companies give you detailed instructions about creating ebooks.

Wonderful Christian self-publishing companies are available to help you publish your book if you choose to go that way. They work similarly to a traditional publisher, except you provide the finances for the book, so there is quite an upfront investment. But for some people, this works very well. If you have a well-known platform and have great opportunity for sales, you could recoup your investment quickly enjoy good sales, as well as have an impact for Christ with your content.

8. **What would be the one thing you would want a new writer to know as he or she is getting started?**

Edna: Forget your five-year plan for success that some secular writers will tell you is essential for your writing career, and spend time praying and meditating on God's Word. Ask Him which part of His plan He wants you to fulfill. Get involved in your local church. Read godly books. Do ministry alongside real saints of God. Give Him the opportunity to show you the world through His eyes. When we seek Him with all our hearts, we can find His will for our writing ministries (Jeremiah 29:13).

The authors would love to hear from you. Let them know how God is directing your writing journey. Email Linda at Linda@lindagilden.com or Edna at Ednae9@aol.com.

Resources to strengthen the leader in you!

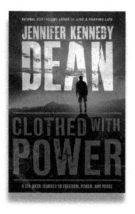

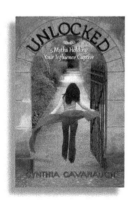

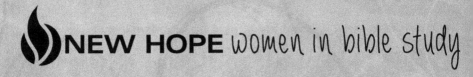